LIVE LIKE YOU BELIEVE

Stories of the Supernatural in Everyday Life

By

Erin Gutowski

All scripture quotations are taken from the New king James Version of the Bible unless otherwise indicated.

Live Like You Believe: Stories of the Supernatural in Everyday Life

ISBN: 978-0-578-93802-8

This book is dedicated to:

My Lord Jesus Christ, the Lover of my soul.

He wrote these stories before the foundation of the world.

May the glory be all to Him.

Table of Contents

PART III: WONDERS

Introduction

I am so excited for you that you decided to delve into the pages of this book!

Here is why: I believe you are seeking something. Maybe you are not a Christian and you have a longing for something more in this life. Maybe you are a Christian, but something still seems to be missing. Perhaps you live with an undercurrent of dissatisfaction or often feel unfulfilled. It's as if you know there is more to this life than what you have experienced so far and you want to find it. Let me tell you my friend, you are absolutely right!

Whether you have no belief in God or have walked in the supernatural with Him all of your life, there is so much more for you to experience in this life! Let me explain how I know this is true.

At the time of writing this book, I had lived more than half of my life NOT believing in God. During those years, I always had a sense that something was missing. I would often think, "Is this all there is to this life?" That thought was very depressing because my life was, well, less than wonderful. In fact, it was very difficult most of the time. I would think, "There has to be more than this…" Yet nothing more ever seemed to come except more pain, more struggle, more depression, more desperation. I began to believe that this was all life had to offer and that nothing would ever change. This belief led me on a path to much depression, discouragement and despair.

When I became a Christian at 29 years old, I knew almost nothing about God, but I believed I had found the "more" I was longing for! As I began my journey into knowing God and believing His Word, I read the Bible, prayed, went to church, watched sermons, read books about God, and attended Christian conferences. As I did all of these things, I found a prominent thought resounding inside my head. It was: "There's more." I would go to bed thinking, "There's more." I would wake up thinking, "There's more."

This went on for years and years. The thought kind of drove me crazy, and yet it also drove me to seek more than what I was experiencing at church and in my daily life. As I continued to seek the Lord, I began to realize that this "voice" was Holy Spirit inviting me into deeper relationship with Him. I have accepted His invitation and have not been disappointed! To this day, He continually invites me, and you, to seek and experience the "more" of Him.

Ask, and it will be given to you; seek, and you shall find: knock, and it will be opened to you. (Matthew 7:7 NKJV)

God is alive and active on planet earth today and He loves to demonstrate His love for all mankind. He shows us in the beauty of a sunset, in the warmth of an autumn breeze, in the coo of a dove, and in all fulness of nature. He also loves to demonstrate His love through miracles, signs and wonders. Experiencing Him in this way requires one thing on your part, you must believe.

All things are possible to him who believes. (Mark 9:23b)

God is supernatural, so for Him to do something supernatural is very natural. As you read this book, you will see just how wonderful, amazing, loving and real God is. Why did these things happen in my life? That's simple. I refused to settle for less than God's best, and I chose to live like I believe the Word of God.

My hope and prayer for you as you read these accounts is that you will be stirred up to seek the "more", believe the Word, and live like you believe.

PART I: MIRACLES

God also bearing witness both with signs and wonders,

with various miracles, and gifts of the Holy Spirit,

according to His own will.

(Hebrews 2:4)

The Bible is an amazing book full of signs, wonders, and miracles. Many people, however, do not believe that it is true. I surely didn't. At the point where I was in my life at 20 years ago, nothing short of a miracle could have convinced me otherwise.

The word *miracles* in Greek is *dynamesin*. It comes from the word *dunamis* which means miraculous power, might, strength. This is where we get the English word *dynamite* from. Used in the plural, as in Heb 2:4, it means powerful deeds, deeds showing (physical) power, or marvelous works.

So, what is a miracle? A miracle is something that happens that is impossible for a human to make happen. It is an occurrence that defies the laws of nature. When you witness or experience a miracle, you know for sure that it was a miracle because you can hardly believe it. Your mind tells you, "That was impossible!" Yet at the same time, you know

5

you just experienced it. In your heart, you know it happened and that it was a miracle!

Why did God perform signs, wonders and miracles? And does He still do them today? The answer to the first question is found in John chapter 20.

Jesus went on to do many more miraculous signs in the presence of his disciples, which are not even included in this book. But all that is recorded here is so that you will fully believe that Jesus is the Anointed One, the Son of God, and that through your faith in him you will experience eternal life by the power of his name! (John 20: 30-31)

God wants all people to fully believe that Jesus is the Son of God and that through believing, each person will experience eternal life. What is eternal life? According to John 17:3, eternal life is NOT living forever. Everyone lives forever.

And this is eternal life, that they may know You, the only true God, and Jesus Christ whom You have sent. (John 17:3)

As for the second question, my answer is YES! The rest of this book will support that belief. What do you believe?

Chapter One: Salvation

Behold, I stand at the door and knock.

If anyone hears My voice and opens the door,

I will come in to him and dine

with him and he with Me.

(Revelation 3:20)

My Beginnings

I was born in Ravenna, Ohio in 1971. My mother and father had grown up in a very small town in northeast Ohio called Kingsville. Though no one else in their families had ever gone to college, they each felt a desire to go. Soon after high school, they married and a few of years later moved to Kent, Ohio to attend Kent State University. A couple of years after that, my sister was born and I came along 20 months after her.

Being so young when they married and each dealing with their own unresolved issues, their marriage did not last. I was 4 years old when they separated, and I truly do not remember much of my life with married parents. From as far back as I can remember, I believed that divorce ruined my life. I decided at a very young age that I would never get divorced.

When I was in 5th grade, my mom moved to another city and my sister went with her. The plan was that I would move with her too when I finished 6th grade, but I never did. The rest of my childhood and teen years were spent living with just my dad. I visited my mom on occasional weekends and during summers, but I had let so much bitterness, anger, and resentment build up in my heart against her that our relationship was mostly painful and ugly.

My dad was a very loving father, but his struggle with alcohol, drugs and women often drew him away mentally and physically. We had no mention of God in our home. We had no Bible, no prayer, no Sunday church visits. I grew up feeling very alone most of the time. I never felt like I fit in anywhere in the extended family or in friend groups at school. I didn't believe in God. I didn't even think about Him or the possibility of Him existing. I didn't really have a reason to, until I was 29 years old.

In January 2001, I was married, had three sons, owned a house, had a car, and was working in the career of my dreams teaching high school math. I was vice-president of the Parent Club at my sons' elementary school, was coaching their sports teams, worked out almost every day, and was finishing up a Master's degree. I had attained everything in life I could possibly think of, and I was absolutely empty and miserable inside.

My marriage was a train wreck. I had a food addiction coupled with an addiction to exercise, which tormented me day and night. I had a warped body image and almost no self-esteem. I was extremely depressed and had no hope. I had put on such a front for others (as least that is what I believed), that I didn't think I could go to anyone for help. Having no belief in God, I was absolutely terrified to die, and yet the thought of living through another day was horrifying.

I remember lying awake in the middle of the night desperately trying to endure the pain of my existence. I felt hopeless and helpless and wondered how I would go on. I silently whispered these words, "God, if you are real, help me..." I did not know it at the time, but this was the first prayer I ever prayed and my life was about to be radically changed!

For "whoever calls on the name of the LORD shall be saved." (Rom 10:13)

Have you ever called on the name of the Lord? Do you believe He would answer if you did? I invite you to live like you believe it and call out to Him.

Saul's Miraculous Encounter

In the book of Acts chapter 7, a man named Saul is introduced. He is consenting to the stoning death of a believer named Stephen. Chapter 8, reveals that Saul hated all Christians and was persecuting the church. Verse 3 says, "As for Saul, he made havoc of the church, entering every house, and dragging off men and women, committing them to prison."

9

I can relate to Saul. There were a handful of times during the period between my high school years and January of 2001 that various people tried to tell me about Jesus. My aunt and one of my friends were believers and tried to talk to me about Jesus. A fellow cub scout leader and his wife made multiple attempts to lead me to the Truth. I am sure there were others that I don't remember.

What I do remember is that I was, let's say, less than kind in letting them know that I was in no way, shape, or form interested in hearing that "garbage". I was rude and adamant about not hearing anything they had to say. Somehow, I had come to believe that religion was created by the government as a means of controlling people. I did not hesitate to share that belief and to bad-mouth those "Jesus freaks" with many curse words.

This seems very strange to me now, but at the time, it was a very real belief. And as you will see, what we hold in our hearts as truth has a dramatic effect on how we live and what we experience in life and in our relationship with God.

For as he thinks in his heart, so is he. (Proverbs 23:7a NKJV)

Here is one of the things that is so amazing about God: He knows your heart better than you do! He knows what you truly believe in the core of your being. He knows how you will respond when He knocks on the door of your heart. He has plans for you according to this foreknowledge.

For I know the plans I have for you," declares the LORD, "plans to prosper you and not to harm you, plans to give you hope and a future. (Jeremiah 29:11 NIV)

10

God knew Saul's heart and how he would respond to the call of God on his life. God had a plan for Saul (who would soon become Paul). All it would take to set this plan in motion was one miracle from God and a response of belief which led to obedience.

Meanwhile, Saul was still breathing out murderous threats against the Lord's disciples. He went to the high priest and asked him for letters to the synagogues in Damascus, so that if he found any there who belonged to the Way, whether men or women, he might take them as prisoners to Jerusalem. As he neared Damascus on his journey, suddenly a light from heaven flashed around him. He fell to the ground and heard a voice say to him, "Saul, Saul, why do you persecute me?" "Who are you, Lord?" Saul asked. (Acts 9: 1-5 NKJV)

Saul's intention was to find Christians and throw them into prison. He had truly believed that this was the right thing to do. Yet one miraculous encounter with Jesus changed the entire trajectory of his life.

In the very moment that Saul experienced the miracle of seeing a light from heaven and hearing God's voice, Saul fully believed that God was real. God knew exactly how Saul would respond. According to verse 5, Saul immediately called Jesus "Lord". He didn't know who He was yet. He didn't know anything about His character, His nature, or the plans He had for Saul, but he knew enough to address Him as Lord. And he believed enough to speak back to that voice! In Acts 26, we find more of this conversation. We also see how God will reveal Himself to you.

> *So I said, 'Who are You, Lord?' And He said, 'I am Jesus, whom you are persecuting. (Acts 26:15)*

One miraculous encounter with Jesus changed Saul's life forever. Do you believe this truly happened? Do you believe this could happen for you? I invite you to believe it!

My Miraculous Encounter

About a month or so after I had prayed that first little prayer of desperation in January of 2001, my whole life was dramatically changed. It was early in the morning and I had woken up, but had not yet opened my eyes. I was home alone because I had been very ill and my husband (at that time) and sons had left for work and school. I was lying in bed having just woken up.

In one split second, brilliant light shone in my mind's eye. The heavens opened before me and I had a glimpse of eternity! It was like nothing I had ever seen or experienced before. I had never felt such love, peace, joy and hope in my entire life. I truly didn't understand what had happened, but I knew two things for sure: God was real and heaven was real. I now understand that what I experienced was a miracle. I saw into the spiritual realm, into heaven! Until that very moment, I did not believe in God or heaven or miracles or anything in the Bible. But that one life-changing encounter, set the trajectory for the rest of my life.

What had truly happened that day? That was the day that I was born again.

Jesus replied, "Very truly I tell you, no one can see the kingdom of God unless they are born again. (John3:3 NIV)

By the power of God, I was translated from the kingdom of darkness into His marvelous light.

that you may proclaim the praises of Him who called you out of darkness into His marvelous light (1 Peter 2:9b NKJV)

It was the moment of my salvation. That day, I became a believer. I was a new creation! I certainly did not understand hardly any of this on that day. Like Saul, I did not know God or Jesus yet. I did not know His character, His nature, His love, His ways, etc. None of these things are requirements for salvation. The only requirement for salvation is that you BELIEVE in your heart and confess with your mouth (Rom 10:9). I didn't even know that, but I immediately called my aunt and my friend to tell them what had happened.

that if you confess with your mouth the Lord Jesus and believe in your heart that God has raised Him from the dead, you will be saved. For with the heart one believes unto righteousness, and with the mouth confession is made unto salvation. For the Scripture says, "Whoever believes on Him will not be put to shame." For there is no distinction between Jew and Greek, for the same Lord over all is rich to all who call upon Him. For "whoever calls on the name of the LORD shall be saved." (Rom 10:9-13)

It only took one miracle to convince Saul to believe and it was the same for me!

13

Not everyone experiences salvation in such a dramatic fashion as Saul and I. Remember, God knows every heart and how each person will respond to His call. He knocks on the heart of every person in a unique way.

Have you ever had an encounter with Jesus? Do you believe that you can? I invite you to live like you believe it.

Should all be saved?

Many people believe that God created some people to go to Heaven and others to go to Hell. This is completely contrary to God's nature and to the Word of God. God's plan and purpose for mankind, His heart toward man and His will for us is clearly laid out in the entirety of scripture. Genesis chapters 1 and 2 show us His heart's desire for mankind and purpose for creation.

Then God said, "Let Us make man in Our image, according to Our likeness; let them have dominion over the fish of the sea, over the birds of the air, and over the cattle, over all the earth and over every creeping thing that creeps on the earth." So God created man in His own image; in the image of God He created him; male and female He created them. Then God blessed them, and God said to them, "Be fruitful and multiply; fill the earth and subdue it; have dominion over the fish of the sea, over the birds of the air, and over every living thing that moves on the earth." (Gen 1:26-28)

God's desire was, and still is, to have children who are like Him, made in His image. God is the creator and ruler of all that exists. He created mankind to be rulers of the earth and all that is within it. This is the reason He said in verse 26 that we would have dominion over all the earth. Dominion is rule and authority. God's desire was, and still is, that his children would be in constant communion with Him, and rule and reign on the earth like He rules and reigns over all. He actually calls us "gods" because we were created to rule the earth.

I said, "You are gods, And all of you are children of the Most High. (Psalm 82:6)

In Genesis chapter 3, we see Adam and Eve hand their God-given authority over to the devil by believing his lies instead of God's truth. Eve entertained a conversation with the devil, and was therefore deceived. Adam obeyed his wife instead of God, submitting himself as a slave to the deceit of the enemy.

Do you not know that to whom you present yourselves slaves to obey, you are that one's slaves whom you obey, whether of sin leading to death, or of obedience leading to righteousness? (Rom 6:16)

When you are believing a lie of the enemy, your words and actions will follow. You present yourself as a slave to sin when you believe the devil's lies. Often, you don't even know you are doing this. The devil is a liar, a deceiver. He deceived Adam and Eve in the Garden and they believed and obeyed him. You will live and obey whatever you believe.

God knew this would happen before he formed the earth or anything on it. Their decision did not change God's heart and plan for mankind. He knew the end from the

15

beginning (Is 46:10). He still desired children made in His image. God is love (1 John 4:8) and love does not demand its own way (1 Cor 13:5). God desires children who, like Him, have the capacity to love. In order for love to be genuine, there must be a choice to love. This is called free will. God created mankind with the capacity to make choices so that they would be able to choose to love God. We all choose what we believe.

Knowing this would happen, God had a plan for redemption for all who would choose to believe in Him. He planned redemption through the death, burial and resurrection of His Son Jesus Christ.

He indeed was foreordained before the foundation of the world, but was manifest in these last times for you who through Him believe in God, who raised Him from the dead and gave Him glory, so that your faith and hope are in God. (1 Peter 1:20-21)

For God so loved the world that He gave His only begotten Son, that whoever believes in Him should not perish but have everlasting life. For God did not send His Son into the world to condemn the world, but that the world through Him might be saved. "He who believes in Him is not condemned; but he who does not believe is condemned already, because he has not believed in the name of the only begotten Son of God. (John 3:16-18)

God's will has never changed. He desires that ALL men would be saved and come to know Him (1 Tim 2:3-4). Scripture is very clear that He does not desire any to perish. We choose our destiny.

And this is eternal life, that they may know You, the only true God, and Jesus Christ whom You have sent. (John 17:3)

The Lord is not slack concerning His promise, as some count slackness, but is longsuffering toward us, not willing that any should perish but that all should come to repentance. (2 Pet 3:9)

God wants all men and women to be saved. Every salvation is a miracle. A person who was spiritually dead becomes spiritually alive. The grace for salvation has been released through the death, burial and resurrection of Jesus for all people. Each person has the choice to believe or not.

For the grace of God that brings salvation has appeared to all men, (Titus 2:11)

Do you believe this could happen to you? Do you believe He created you to go to heaven? I invite you to believe it and receive Him right now.

If you have never received Jesus as your Lord and savior, you can do so right now. You can say your own declaration of belief according to Rom 10:9 or pray these words:

Father God, I know that I am a sinner in need of a savior. I believe that Jesus is Your only begotten Son and that He died on the cross for all of my sins. I confess with my mouth that I believe You raised Him from the dead. Thank you for saving me! Thank you that I am now Your child! I want to live the rest of my life for you and with you! Thank you that Your Holy Spirit now lives in me and will lead and guide me into all the truth! Thank Holy Father. Amen!

Chapter Two: Freedom

Then Jesus said to those Jews who believed Him,

"If you abide in My word, you are My disciples

indeed.

And you shall know the truth,

and the truth shall make you free."

(John 8:31-32)

Becoming a Disciple

I graduated from high school in 1989 and soon found out I was pregnant. I gave birth to my first son when I was 18 years old and married his father at 20. We had two more sons by the time I turned 23. We were young, lost, and hurting souls. We were both non-believers when we got together, and without God, any relationship will struggle to survive. Many ungodly behaviors plagued the relationship. After I got saved, the marriage got even worse because my husband was not willing to invite Jesus into our home, but I was.

Before the day of my salvation in January 2001, I was extremely depressed, even suicidal. The moment I got saved,

19

I experienced great peace, joy and hope like I had never experienced before. I had become a new creation.

Therefore, if anyone is in Christ, he is a new creation; old things have passed away; behold, all things have become new. (2 Cor 5:17)

Before that day, I was spiritually dead. I was a soul (a mind, will, emotions, conscience, personality) in a physical body. On the day of my salvation, I became a three-part being with a spirit, a soul, and a body (1 Thes 5:23). The Holy Spirit came to live inside of me and made me spiritually alive. This creation had never existed before (2 Cor 5:17). I discovered a new desire in my heart to read the Bible. I found a new desire in my heart to pray. I had a new desire in my heart to get to know this Jesus who had saved me.

Soon after I got saved, I acquired a Bible and read it straight through from Genesis to Revelation. I had no idea that it was not in chronological order. I did not know that the Old Testament needed to be read in light of the finished work of the cross. I had had no Biblical teaching, no church experience, and no idea how to pray, but I had faith. God had placed His faith inside of me on the day I believed (Gal 2:20).

I believed every word I read even though I didn't understand much of it. The love of God had been poured into my heart (Rom 5:5) and was drawing me to Himself. He wanted me to know and experience Him more.

For this is good and acceptable in the sight of God our Savior, who desires all men to be saved and to come to the knowledge of the truth. (1 Tim 2:3-4)

After the day I got saved, I was on a spiritual high for weeks. As the days and weeks went by, however, the reality of my current circumstances set in. I was different, but nothing in my physical world had changed. I still had a horrible marriage, painful memories, bad relationships, food and exercise addictions, body-image issues, etc. I was still experiencing great desperation, anxiety and depression.

Having read the Bible, I starting believing there was more to life than what I was experiencing. I had hope for the future that I didn't have before. The problem was that I was not *experiencing* what I believed was possible and I didn't understand why. As with all things that we don't understand, the Word of God will reveal the answer.

God does not just want all men to be saved, He also wants us to come to the knowledge of the truth. It is the truth, and only the truth, which makes us free. Many Christians receive salvation, but never walk in the freedom that Christ paid for them to have (Gal 5:1). In order to experience the freedom, a believer must become a disciple.

Then Jesus said to those Jews who believed Him, "If you abide in My word, you are My disciples indeed. And you shall know the truth, and the truth shall make you free."
(John 8:31-32)

I decided to continue in the Word. Day after day, I would read the Bible. I pursued God with my whole heart. After all, He was the one who ripped me up out of the darkness and showed me His marvelous light!

I had read in the Bible that He would never leave me nor forsake me (Heb 13:5). Somehow, I believed this even though many times it felt like He was not there. He said He wouldn't leave, so I kept talking to Him like He was still there. I also read that truth would make me free (John 8:31-32) and that Jesus IS truth (John 14:6). I was not yet living free from depression, so I knew that I needed to know Jesus more. I knew He was my Savior, but I didn't know much more about Him.

I started going to church to learn more about Him and to be around others who believed in Him. I began to pray and to journal out prayers. I copied scriptures into my journal day after day, scripture after scripture, page after page. The Word drew me in and created a stronger and stronger desire inside of me to KNOW Him. The more I knew, the more I wanted to know.

I began reading books by Joyce Meyer, A.W. Tozer, Francis Chan, Stormie Omartian, C.S. Lewis, Henry Blackaby, Rick Warren, John Ortberg, Max Lucado and many others. I wanted to know everything anyone else knew about Jesus. I went to church whenever it was open and attended conferences wherever the Word was preached. I just HAD to know this Jesus who saved my life!

The Word of God is seed (Mark 4:14). If you plant it in your heart it will grow. Just like seeds in the physical realm, seeds of truth in the spiritual realm take time to grow. Lies are also seeds that take root in a heart and grow. Some of the things I read and heard were true, others were not. As a baby Christian, I did not know the difference. What I have since learned is that the truth is far more powerful than the lies.

He put another parable before them, saying, "The kingdom of heaven may be compared to a man who sowed good seed in his field, but while his men were sleeping, his enemy came and sowed weeds among the wheat and went away. So when the plants came up and bore grain, then the weeds appeared also. And the servants of the master of the house came and said to him, 'Master, did you not sow good seed in your field? How then does it have weeds?' He said to them, 'An enemy has done this.' So the servants said to him, 'Then do you want us to go and gather them?' But he said, 'No, lest in gathering the weeds you root up the wheat along with them. Let both grow together until the harvest, and at harvest time I will tell the reapers, "Gather the weeds first and bind them in bundles to be burned, but gather the wheat into my barn." (Matthew 13:24-30)

In this parable, Jesus was teaching that we need to sow good seed, the Word, into our hearts. The enemy will sow weeds through lies and false doctrine. Both truth and lies will produce fruit of beliefs which lead to behaviors. Truth produces good fruit/behavior and lies produce bad fruit/behavior. Jesus was not concerned about them growing together because He knew that in the end the lies and their fruit would be burned up.

As I sought truth with my whole heart, I continued planting good seed in my heart by abiding in the Word (John 8:31-32). The lies that were planted along the way were being exposed and weeded out. I had become a disciple and the truth was making me free. The Word is alive and powerful (Heb 4:12) and it was working in me (Phil 2:13). My desperation,

23

anxiety and despair were slowly being replaced with hope, peace, and joy.

Are there lies you are believing that are keeping you worried, anxious and depressed? Do you believe that Bible is the truth? Do you believe the truth will set you free from all of this? I invite you to believe it and live like you do!

Freedom from Destruction

Four years after I was saved, my marriage ended in a long and painful divorce. I was 33 years old. I had believed in my heart that my parents' divorce ruined my life, so I had made that declaration in my heart as a child to never get divorced. I now see how this vow helped cause great pain and suffering for my children, my ex-husband, and myself.

Seeds that are planted in a little child's mind often grow very deep roots in the heart. I had decided as a child that when I grew up I would create the family I never had. That was a wonderful idea, but apart from Christ, I could not accomplish that goal (John 15:5). So, going through the divorce was like going through a death. It was the death of everything I had dreamed of and tried to create but couldn't.

The other "death" I experienced was death of the façade I had created in mind that everything was "ok" and that everything would get better. Two very broken people, without Jesus, will never create something beautiful and whole. The pain of facing the reality of the situation was almost unbearable. The truth was that I had helped to create a volatile marriage which caused great damage to myself, my children and my ex-husband. I had also helped to keep us all in the situation for way too many years.

Ending that marriage was pain like I had never experienced before. Ungodly soul ties were being severed and the devil was working overtime to not allow that to happen. I physically could not eat or sleep for weeks. I held on to the Word by faith and He held on to me. I was keenly aware of a great spiritual battle going on in and around me and yet I had no strength to fight it. During this time, I read continually in the book of Psalms and also encountered the story of David.

David is first mentioned in the Bible in 1 Samuel 16. He was chosen by God to be king of Israel and deemed "a man after God's own heart." (Acts 13:22). The history of David continues through 2 Samuel. David does many heroic and honorable things by faith in the Lord. Nevertheless, in 2 Samuel 11, we find David making bad choices which cause destruction to himself and many others.

It happened in the spring of the year, at the time when kings go out to battle, that David sent Joab and his servants with him, and all Israel; and they destroyed the people of Ammon and besieged Rabbah. But David remained at Jerusalem. Then it happened one evening that David arose from his bed and walked on the roof of the king's house. And from the roof he saw a woman bathing, and the woman was very beautiful to behold. So David sent and inquired about the woman. And someone said, "Is this not Bathsheba, the daughter of Eliam, the wife of Uriah the Hittite?" Then David sent messengers, and took her; and she came to him, and he lay with her, for she was cleansed from her impurity; and she returned to her house. And the

woman conceived; so she sent and told David, and said,
"I am with child." (2 Sam 11:1-5)

It was the time when kings go out to battle, yet David was home. He was married, but decided to inquire about a beautiful woman. After he learned that she was a married woman, he followed temptation into sin, which produced a child. David tried to cover up his sin by luring the woman's husband, Uriah, home from war to sleep with his wife to make it appear that the baby was his. When his plan failed, David devised a new plan which resulted in Uriah's death. (2 Sam 11:6-17). After Bathsheba mourned her husband's death, David took her as his wife. (2 Sam 11:26-27) The child they had conceived died shortly after birth.

David was a "man after God's own heart", yet his choices caused destruction and pain to himself and others. He chose to be unfaithful in his own marriage and also caused a married woman to sin. He caused the deaths of an innocent man and of an innocent child. I felt like David when I ended my marriage. I loved the Lord with all my heart, but I had made many choices that created much pain and destruction to myself and to others.

As I read Psalm after Psalm, I saw David's heart and God's great love and mercy for him. I also began to believe in God's great love and mercy for me. I learned that He forgave all my iniquities and redeemed my life even from the destruction I caused.

Bless the LORD, O my soul,
And forget not all His benefits:
Who forgives all your iniquities,

Who heals all your diseases,
Who redeems your life from destruction,
Who crowns you with lovingkindness and tender mercies,
(Psa 103:2-4)

The LORD also will be a refuge for the oppressed,
A refuge in times of trouble.
And those who know Your name will put their trust in You;
For You, LORD, have not forsaken those who seek You (Psa
9:9-10)

But I have trusted in Your mercy;
My heart shall rejoice in Your salvation.
I will sing to the LORD,
Because He has dealt bountifully with me. (Psa 13:5-6)

Therefore my heart is glad, and my glory rejoices;
My flesh also will rest in hope.
For You will not leave my soul in Sheol,
Nor will You allow Your Holy One to see corruption.
You will show me the path of life;
In Your presence is fullness of joy;
At Your right hand are pleasures forevermore. (Psa 16:9-11)

I will love You, O LORD, my strength.
The LORD is my rock and my fortress and my deliverer;
My God, my strength, in whom I will trust;
My shield and the horn of my salvation, my stronghold. (Psa
18:1-2)

The LORD will give strength to His people;
The LORD will bless His people with peace. (Psa 29:11)

27

These are just a few of the numerous verses that caused me to believe that regardless of my past decisions, God loved me and had a plan to deliver me and my children from the destruction I had helped to cause.

David repented of his sin and turned back to the Lord in 2 Sam 12. The Lord restored David and Bathsheba, giving them another child, Solomon, whom the Lord loved. (2 Sam 12:24). God also kept a covenant He made with David, not because David did everything right, but because God keeps His word (2 Sam 7:12-16).

God is no respecter of persons. (Acts 10:34). He did it for David, and I believed He would to do it for me. Because I believed this, I began to live like I was forgiven. I believed God did not want me to live in the pain and guilt from the destruction I had caused. I began to seek this freedom in the Word.

Are there things you have done in your life that have caused destruction to you or to others? Have others done things to you that have caused destruction? Do you believe that God has forgiven you and that He can heal and restore all that has been done? I invite you to believe it and live like you do!

Freedom from Depression

As I continued reading the Bible, I encountered the truth (John 14:6). As I continued in other books, conferences, churches, and teachings, I encountered truth mixed with lies (bad doctrine and unbelief). However, the power of the truth is much greater that the power of any lie. Read John 8:31-32 again.

> *Then Jesus said to those Jews who believed Him, "If you abide in My word, you are My disciples indeed. And you shall know the truth, and the truth shall make you free."*
> *(John 8:31-32)*

Read it slowly. There are five important components. First, Jesus was speaking to believers. They already BELIEVED. He offered these believers a **choice**. He said "IF you abide in My word. You are my disciples indeed." The word "if" is used in conditional statements. A conditional statement includes two parts. The first part is the condition (hypothesis) which may or may not be fulfilled. If the condition is fulfilled, the second part of the statement, the result (conclusion), is *guaranteed* to happen.

This is where free will comes in. These Jews had made the first, most important free-will decision every human is invited to make (Rom 10:9-10). They had chosen to believe that Jesus is who He says He is. But then Jesus was offering the next most important free-will decision. They now had to make the choice to abide (remain; stay; continue; dwell) in His Word or not. If they chose to abide in His Word, they would become disciples, not just converts.

Each of us who has made the choice to believe in Jesus has become a convert. We have converted from non-believers to believers, from the kingdom of darkness to the Kingdom of Light. And yet, there is another choice to make. Jesus invites us to become disciples and even tells us how to do this – abide

29

in His Word. In fact, this is His heart's desire. This is the will of God. Recall 1 Tim 2:3-4.

For this is good and acceptable in the sight of God our Savior, who desires all men to be saved and to come to the knowledge of the truth. (1 Tim 2:3-4)

God wants us to be saved AND come to the knowledge of truth. Jesus did not just come to pay for your ticket to heaven. He came to destroy all the works of the enemy (1 John 3:8). He came to save us AND set us free from the prisons of sin. Once you are a disciple, you will begin to know the truth. When you know truth in you heart, not just in your head, it makes you free.

Many Christians want to skip from step one to step three. This is called pride. Pride is doing things your own way, not God's way. Jesus lays out the three steps very clearly in John 8:31-32. First, become a convert by believing. Next, become a disciple by abiding. Third, be set free by knowing truth.

I am a living testimony that His plan works. As I continued in the Word for days, weeks and years I knew more and more truth. Desperation, guilt, anxiety, worry and depression were over-taken by love, joy, peace and hope. The more I knew God, His goodness, His love, His mercy, His forgiveness, His grace, His peace, His joy, His plan for my life, there was just no space in my heart for anxiety and fear. I became free from depression!

Anxiety in the heart of man causes depression, But a good word makes it glad. (Prov 12:25)

30

Do you often experience anxiety, worry and depression? Do you believe the Word of God will take it away from you? Are you willing to abide in His Word and let it work in you? I encourage you to believe that the Word will work and take a step to abide in Him!

Freedom from Heartbreak

Two years after my divorce, I entered into a brutal custody battle which ensued for almost two years. In the end, my two youngest sons wanted to live with their dad and the courts conceded. I remember the exact moment I found out I had lost the battle.

It was a Tuesday night and I had gone to church for a women's Bible study. The boys were at their dad's house for visitation. After the study, I came out of the church, got into my car, and checked a voice message on my phone. I heard my ex-husband say "I got custody. The boys are not coming home." I honestly think I was in shock at that very moment. I do not remember anything until the next morning. Somehow, I made it home, called off work for the next day, and collapsed into bed.

Losing my children took emotional pain to a level I never imagined I could possibly survive. The morning after that phone message, I remember waking up and having no strength or desire to do anything. I had a broken heart, literally. I felt such emotional pain in such a physical way that it is hard to describe. It was like my heart had physically

31

shattered in a million pieces so that it was even difficult to breathe.

I sat in my bed and sobbed and sobbed until there were no tears left in my body. I was exhausted and yet one prominent thought became very clear. I knew at that moment that I had come to life-determining cross road. I had a decision to make that would set the course of the rest of my life. Either God was good or He was not.

I could choose to look at all the evidence in the physical realm to make this decision. After all, I was a Christian and my ex-husband was not. I had had an entire team of prayer warriors praying for me and the kids for two years. Thoughts tried to come in like, "How could God let this happen?" and "How could this be God's will?' and "What did I do wrong?" and "How will I go on without them?"

As I look back on that day 13 years ago, I see the grace of God and the power of the Holy Spirit working together in my life. Though I did not know then what was happening, it was Holy Spirit who brought that life-directing ultimatum to my mind. And by the grace of God, I made the right decision.

I determined in my heart that day that God is good. This may sound trite, but once I settled that in my heart, every single circumstance in my life had to be filtered through that truth. This declaration that God is good, became an immutable heart position. From that moment on, no matter what was going on in my life, I would never abandon my faith in Him or doubt His goodness. This meant that if a circumstance tried to convince me that God was not good, then the circumstance was lying.

The power of believing this one simple truth set me on the path for healing from the heartbreak.

"So I will restore to you the years that the swarming locust has eaten, (Joel 2:25a)

Have you ever had your heart broken? Have you ever thought that the emotional pain of your situation was too much for you to endure? Do you believe that God desires to deliver you and heal you from all this pain? I encourage you to believe it and receive this healing today.

PART II: SIGNS

God also bearing witness both with

signs and wonders, with various miracles,

and gifts of the Holy Spirit,

according to His own will.

(Hebrews 2:4)

God is in the business of making Himself known on the earth. He desires that people would know Him personally and intimately. He uses various methods to convince people that He exists. Believing that He exists is the first step in getting to know Him. After the miracle of salvation happens in a person's life, he or she is invited into the journey of coming to know and experience God in so many ways. Each person has the choice of the extent to which he or she gets to know Him.

But without faith it is impossible to please Him, for he who comes to God must believe that He is, and that He is a rewarder of those who diligently seek Him. (Hebrews 11:6)

The middle part of Hebrews 11:6 says that he who comes to God must BELIEVE that He is. That is what happens at salvation. But there is more! The last part says that He is a rewarded of those who diligently seek Him. Do you believe this?

What if a man you never met before came to your door and told you he had buried a million dollars in your back yard? What would you do? Your action would be directly related to what you believe to be true in that moment. If you believed the man, you would probably go get a shovel (or a back hoe) and start digging! If you did not believe him, you would do nothing.

The Bible says God is a rewarder of those who *diligently* seek Him (Heb 11:6). Now, I am not saying pursue God to get rewards. What I *am* saying is that *if* you diligently seek Him, He rewards you. The Word says so.

One of the many rewards I have been given by God are signs. The Greek word for "sign" is *semeion*. It means a sign given especially to confirm, corroborate or authenticate with the end purpose of exalting the one giving it. God gives us signs to bear witness of His goodness and confirm things in our lives for us.

He is an intimate God. John 15:5 tells us that we can do nothing apart from Him. The good news is that as a believer, you are never apart from Him! We were never created to be separate from Him, nor to do anything without Him.

Do you believe you have ever received a sign from God? I invite you to believe that He is rewarding you right now as you seek Him by reading this book!

36

Chapter Three: Provision

"Therefore do not be like them.

For your Father knows the things you

have need of before you ask Him.

(Matthew 6:8)

Help

Sometimes the best prayers are the shortest ones. In January of 2008, I was at the tail end of the custody battle for my two youngest sons. I was exhausted and feeling like I could not keep fighting the battle. I was tired, out of money, emotionally drained and considering just giving up. I remember one distinct moment of surrender. In that moment, I threw myself onto the couch, buried my face in my hands and cried out to God. Here was my eloquent prayer: "God, I need help!"

In my distress I called upon the LORD,
And cried out to my God;
He heard my voice from His temple,
And my cry came before Him, even to His ears. (Psalm 18:6)

A few weeks later, a friend of mine invited me to go to a Christian concert with her and her husband. She had front row tickets and the band was one I really enjoyed. It was out of character for me to spend money on a concert ticket, but for some reason I said yes.

After I had agreed to go, she informed me that her husband and his twin brother were also going. I had been introduced to her brother-in-law once at church, but I couldn't even remember what he looked like and truly didn't care who was going. I was just excited to go out and have some fun, which was something I hadn't done in years. I was NOT in the business of dating, and was holding fast to my conviction to NEVER be married again!

On February 16, 2008, we all met up at my friend's house before going out to dinner. I did not know that we would be going into her house first, and that I would have to take off my shoes. I had worn socks with holes in them! When I came into her living room, I sat on my feet so no one would see the holes. It actually was strange to me that I even cared what they thought of my socks. As the night went on, I noticed more and more little thoughts that were different than I was used to.

As we were walking to the restaurant, the brother-in-law, Mitchell, offered his arm to help me across some ice. I promptly said, "No, thank you. I don't need help." At dinner, I noticed that I was too embarrassed to even look Mitchell in the face. I was strangely uncomfortable around him and beginning to feel some kind of attraction. I was NOT pleased with these feelings because of my vow to never date or be married again. I kept trying to reject all of the thoughts coming into my head and the feelings stirring in my heart.

During the concert, the main singer invited us to sit down to pray. My friend had strategically placed me next to Mitchell. As we sat down, I leaned forward placing my elbows on my knees and my face in my hands. I intentionally leaned my right knee outward just enough to touch his. At the moment our knees touched, a surge of power shot through my body! It felt like electricity and froze me in my seat! I thought, "What was that?!"

I am still not exactly sure what it was, but I know this much, it was a sign from God. Two weeks after the concert, Mitchell told me that he was going to marry me, to which I promptly said, "Don't ever say that again!" I had a lot of fear and past hurts, but God had a plan.

For I know the plans I have for you," declares the LORD, "plans to prosper you and not to harm you, plans to give you hope and a future. (Jeremiah 29:11 NIV)

I had prayed for help. I needed hope for my future. God wanted to prosper me and not have my past continue to harm me. God knew I needed a husband who would love and cherish me. I needed a husband to lead and protect me. I needed a husband to help restore me to the fullness of who God created me to be. I didn't know what I needed beyond "help", but God knew.

Over the next five and a half months, the Lord worked in my heart to believe and receive the "help" I needed. I had a group of faithful women who loved the Lord and prayed for me as I cried each week about this developing relationship. I was so afraid to enter into another relationship where I could get deeply wounded again.

After a few months of this sniveling, one of my friends said, "Erin, what if you just let go of all fear?" I guess I had never thought of that. Fear will paralyze you and stop you from entering into God's plan for your life. It is amazing how God will send you someone to speak a life-changing question or truth into your heart.

After she spoke those words, I thought, "What if I just did that...?" I distinctly remember the time and place where I let go of all fear. I was at a retreat in a little room all alone. I buried my face in my hands, slid down the corner of a wall, and imagined that I was letting go of all fear.

In my mind, I saw myself falling, but not fast. It was dark, but not scary. I kept gently falling and falling until I eventually landed softly, into the middle of the Lord's hands. At that moment I heard, "This is the man I have for you for the rest of your life." And in that moment, I BELIEVED that it was true.

> *My sheep hear My voice, and I know them, and they*
> *follow Me. (John 10:27)*

The Lord speaks to us in many different ways. When He called me to marry Mitchell, He gave me a vision and a complete sentence in my spirit. This is similar to Ananias, the man who was sent to Saul right after his conversion in Acts 9.

> *Now there was a certain disciple at Damascus named*
> *Ananias; and to him the Lord said in a vision, "Ananias."*
> *And he said, "Here I am, Lord." So the Lord said to*
> *him, "Arise and go to the street called Straight, and inquire*
> *at the house of Judas for one called Saul of Tarsus, for*
> *behold, he is praying. And in a vision he has seen a man*

40

named Ananias coming in and putting his hand on him, so that he might receive his sight." (Acts 9:10-12)

God knew how Saul would respond when He called to Him. He also knew what Saul would need to move forward in the plan He had for Saul to become Paul. God knew how I would respond to Him when He spoke to me about Mitchell. He knew what I needed to become the real me.

Mitchell and I were married a few months later on August 29, 2008. The adventure was about to begin! Thirteen years later, I am fully convinced God knew what I needed before I even asked (Matt 6:8).

Do you believe that God wants to help you in every situation? Do you believe that God knows what you need and has a good plan for your life? I believe He does! I invite you to believe it and ask Him for help and a vision of His plan right now.

Spiritual Hearing

In January of 2010 a magnitude 7.0 earthquake devastated the nation of Haiti. Mitchell and I both perceived the Lord was sending us there to help. Mitchell had been on two mission trips before we met and I had been on one. We had a heart for missions and gladly said "yes" to the Lord. We spent half the summer serving in Haiti with a mission organization and truly encountered the life-changing love of God.

In Haiti, we learned how to intentionally listen for Holy Spirit's leading each and every day. Every mission team member would get up each morning and spend time alone in prayer and worship with Holy Spirit. We would then come together for corporate prayer and worship. During those times, Holy Spirit would reveal His plan for us for the day. We would go wherever the Spirit led us.

> *Commit to the LORD whatever you do, and he will establish your plans. (Proverbs 16:3)*

The Lord truly established our plans each and every day. He confirmed His Word with signs as He promises. We saw healings, demons cast out, hearts renewed and hope restored.

> *And these signs will follow those who believe: In My name they will cast out demons; they will speak with new tongues; they will take up serpents; and if they drink anything deadly, it will by no means hurt them; they will lay hands on the sick, and they will recover." (Mark 16:17-18)*

When we arrived back in the states, we both felt a call to missions. Together we declared, "We are missionaries for You, Lord. Send us wherever, whenever." We were standing in agreement. We truly believed God had called us to this.

> *"Again I say to you that if two of you agree on earth concerning anything that they ask, it will be done for them by My Father in heaven. (Matthew 18:19)*

We spent the next two years preparing our hearts and our house for a move. I began purging every unnecessary thing we owned and Mitchell began fixing whatever needed to be fixed on the house. We didn't care where we were going; we just knew we had to go. Because we believed, we took steps of faith in the direction we felt God leading us. Faith without works is dead (Jas 2). When you truly believe you have heard from the Lord, you will take a corresponding step of faith.

In February of 2012, we heard the answer to our prayer. The Lord told us to move to Chicago. We had no idea why, what we would do there, where we would work, where we would go to church, nor any other details. We just knew He said, "Move to Chicago." (John 10:27)

When He called us to Haiti, both of us had a desire and a "knowing" in our hearts that we were supposed to go. We see in Romans 8 that the Holy Spirit will lead us and "bear witness" with our spirit.

For as many as are led by the Spirit of God, these are sons of God. For you did not receive the spirit of bondage again to fear, but you received the Spirit of adoption by whom we cry out, "Abba, Father." The Spirit Himself bears witness with our spirit that we are children of God, (Rom 8:14-16)

When He called us to Chicago, He gave me a three-day encounter with Him which included visions and spiritual conversations. It was similar to the story of Peter when the Lord was convincing him to take the gospel to the Gentiles, not just the Jews.

The next day, as they went on their journey and drew near the city, Peter went up on the housetop to pray, about the sixth hour. Then he became very hungry and

43

wanted to eat; but while they made ready, he fell into a trance and saw heaven opened and an object like a great sheet bound at the four corners, descending to him and let down to the earth. In it were all kinds of four-footed animals of the earth, wild beasts, creeping things, and birds of the air. And a voice came to him, "Rise, Peter; kill and eat." But Peter said, "Not so, Lord! For I have never eaten anything common or unclean." And a voice spoke to him again the second time, "What God has cleansed you must not call common." This was done three times. And the object was taken up into heaven again. (Acts 10: 9-16)

When you become a believer, the Spirit of God comes to live inside of you. (Romans 5:5) At that very moment, you are given all things that you will ever need to live a life of godliness through His divine power in you. Spiritual hearing is included in "all things".

as His divine power has given to us all things that pertain to life and godliness, through the knowledge of Him who called us by glory and virtue, (2 Peter 1:3)

We access all of these things "through the knowledge of Him". This is called relationship. Recall that God's desire is that all would be saved and come to the knowledge of Him (1 Tim 2:3-4). He desires this for you because knowing Him is knowing truth (John 14:6) and truth, when you KNOW it makes you free (John 8:32).

Jesus came to set you free from all effects of sin (Gal 5:1), all the works of the devil (1 John 3:8) and all things that would keep you from enjoying fellowship and communion

44

with Him (1 John 1:3). In order to fellowship with God and get to know Him, you need to hear His voice.

Think about your relationship with your best friend. You were not best friends the first moment you met. You started as acquaintances and became friends over time by hanging out, doing things together, and talking. The more you got to know each other, the stronger the friendship grew.

Once you became close friends, the desire to spend time together didn't go away, it grew stronger. You still desired to know this person more and experience more of life with him or her. This is how relationships work with humans and also with God. There is commitment and an investment of time involved in developing and maintaining good relationships with people and with the Jesus.

God wants to spend time with you. In fact, He desires this so much that He never leaves you (Heb 13:5). He wants you to spend all of your time with Him. God wants you to get to know Him (John 17:3). Because of His desire for you, He has placed in you the ability to hear His voice. This ability is a gift and it is perfect.

Every good gift and every perfect gift is from above, and comes down from the Father of lights, with whom there is no variation or shadow of turning. (James 1:17)

Spiritual hearing is a good and perfect gift given to you by God on the day you got saved. You can hear God (John 10:27). Many Christians say, "God is not speaking to me." or, "I have never heard God." I even said those things myself until I learned that I was believing lies. As I spent time in His Word, God revealed this truth to me and it set me free.

When a baby is born, he has ears. No one needs to teach the baby how to hear. Those ears know how to hear. When a sound occurs within the baby's hearing range, the baby hears the sound. He doesn't have to try to hear the sound. His ears pick up the sound because that is what ears do by nature. Now, the baby might not know what the sound is, but he hears the sound nonetheless.

As the child grows, he begins to distinguish sounds. He learns which sound is the dog barking, the doorbell ringing, the vacuum cleaner, his sister singing, etc. This is also how our spiritual hearing works. You are born-again with the ability to hear God's voice. He is continually speaking and you are hearing, but as a new believer, you may not recognize His voice.

As you spend time getting to know Him through His Word and His Spirit, you will begin to discern His voice. The journey of discerning His voice begins with believing that He already gave you this perfect gift of hearing and that you do hear Him. Once you sincerely believe those truths, you will begin to recognize His voice.

The journey of discerning His voice never ends. God desires your relationship with Him to grow deeper each and every day you are alive in this world. A human parent would not speak to a five-year-old the same way he would speak to a teenager. This is also true in our relationship with God. As we grow in the knowledge of Him, He speaks to us in more mature ways.

of whom we have much to say, and hard to explain,
since you have become dull of hearing. For though by this

time you ought to be teachers, you need someone to teach you again the first principles of the oracles of God; and you have come to need milk and not solid food. For everyone who partakes only of milk is unskilled in the word of righteousness, for he is a babe. But solid food belongs to those who are of full age, that is, those who by reason of use have their senses exercised to discern both good and evil. (Hebrews 5:11-14)

God has given us the ability to hear Him, however we must not become dull of hearing. We need to renew our minds by the Word (Romans 12:2), encourage each other daily (Heb 13:3), remain in fellowship with Him (John 15:4), and allow Holy Spirit to guide us into all truth (John 16:13). He desires that we grow in the knowledge of Him and learn to discern His voice above all others.

but grow in the grace and knowledge of our Lord and Savior Jesus Christ. To Him be the glory both now and forever. Amen. (2 Peter 3:18)

Do you believe that God speaks to you? Do you believe that you hear Him? When you truly believe the first part of John 10:27, the second part will come true; you will follow Him! I invite you to live like you believe. Ask Holy Spirit to help you discern His voice and hear Him above all other voices.

Things to Come

Right before we moved from Ohio to Chicago, Mitchell kept telling me, "Erin, I see land. Lots and lots of land". My husband is quite the visionary, so I knew what he meant. The Lord was showing him things to come. Jesus promises us that Holy Spirit will do this.

However, when He, the Spirit of truth, has come, He will guide you into all truth; for He will not speak on His own authority, but whatever He hears He will speak; and He will tell you things to come. (John 16:13)

God did this same thing with Abram, whose name was later changed to Abraham. He was calling him out of the land where he and all of his family lived. He chose Abram, spoke to him, gave him a promise, and invitation to follow Him.

Now the LORD had said to Abram: "Get out of your country, From your family And from your father's house, To a land that I will show you. I will make you a great nation; I will bless you And make your name great; And you shall be a blessing. I will bless those who bless you, And I will curse him who curses you; And in you all the families of the earth shall be blessed." (Genesis 12:1-3)

Abram "departed as the Lord had spoken to him" (Gen 12:4). Because he believed God, Abram took a step of obedience by faith. After his step of obedience, the Lord revealed more to him.

Then the LORD appeared to Abram and said, "To your descendants I will give this land." And there he built an altar to the LORD, who had appeared to him. (Genesis 12:7)

Abram continued believing God and therefore, kept taking steps. God continued to reveal move of His plan to him.

And the LORD said to Abram, after Lot had separated from him: "Lift your eyes now and look from the place where you are—northward, southward, eastward, and westward; for all the land which you see I give to you and your descendants forever. And I will make your descendants as the dust of the earth; so that if a man could number the dust of the earth, then your descendants also could be numbered. Arise, walk in the land through its length and its width, for I give it to you." (Genesis 14:14-17)

Abram continued believing and obeying. God upheld His promise to show Abram the land (Gen 12:1). Abram did not do everything perfectly, but that is not what God requires. Faith pleases God (Heb 11:6), not perfection. Abram believed God and it was accounted to him as righteousness (Gen 15:6).

When God speaks to you, it is always an invitation to follow Him in His perfect will and plan for you. It is an invitation into intimacy and dependence upon Him. You always have a choice. God will never force you to do anything. Love does not demand its own way (1 Cor 13:5). When you truly believe you heard from God AND believe He has only good planned for you, you will take a step of obedience.

49

I truly believed Mitchell had "heard" from God in a vision. I believed He had shown him things to come. The problem I had with Mitchell's vision, was that I had a different one. I kept seeing people, lots and lots of people. When Mitchell talked about his vision, all I could see was the two of us sitting in rocking chairs, staring across acres of emptiness, rocking away into nothingness. It was a horrible thought to me. I knew the problem was in my mind.

I decided to ask God what was going on. I said, "Lord, I KNOW you put us together. I mean, it was not MY idea to ever get married again. I asked for help. You gave me a husband. You said, 'This is the man I have for you for the rest of your life.' I believed You. This was YOUR plan. Now You are giving him one vision and giving me a different vision, but that is not what You do. You don't call people together to separate them. And You said, 'Move to Chicago'. That's not land. We can literally touch the house on either side of us just standing between them. Please show me how this all fits together."

Then you will call upon Me and go and pray to Me,
and I will listen to you. And you will seek Me and
find Me, when you search for Me with all your heart.
(Jeremiah 29:12-13)

As my relationship with God grew deeper, I began to pray differently. Just like any other relationship, as you grow closer, you talk differently. You become more comfortable, open and honest. As I began to know and understand more of God's character and nature, I was able to approach Him from a place of honesty and trust.

I knew He was the Giver of good gifts, not the destroyer. His heart is unity, not division. I knew I didn't have to throw myself into a chair and have a baby fit any more. I just simply needed to ask in faith, believe He would answer, and listen for His response. He tells you things to come (John 16:13) and He promises to answer when you ask.

Ask, and it will be given to you; seek, and you will find; knock, and it will be opened to you. For everyone who asks receives, and he who seeks finds, and to him who knocks it will be opened. (Matt 7:7-8)

The Lord surely answered. He showed me how the land was going to be a place of ministry where the "lots and lots" of people would come. He showed me that Chicago was a training ground, not a stopping place. It all made sense, as it always does when we allow Him to show us the plan. I didn't know all the details, in fact very few, but it was all I needed to know.

We moved in 2012 carrying the vision with us, believing we needed to be trained and prepared for what was to come. Looking back on our years in Chicago, we can see how much we learned and grew in relationship with God, with each other, and with people. We would have never had that opportunity had we not stepped out in faith to follow Him.

Has God ever shown you things to come? Do you believe that He will? I invite you to believe He will, ask Him to do it, and receive all He has for you right now.

Open Doors

God spoke "Chicago" to me on February 18, 2012. The Lord had told me during a three-day miraculous encounter with Him that we would be moving in August. This meant that we only had five and a half months to sell a house, buy a house, quit a job, find jobs, transfer my teaching license and all the other things required to move to another state. From the moment we believed we had heard God's direction, we began to take steps toward Chicago. Faith has feet.

On February 28, I discovered that there were two bogus claims on our credit report causing our credit score to show considerably lower than it actually was. This would have caused our new mortgage payment to be much higher than it should be. I called to find out what I needed to do to get these false claims removed. I took the necessary steps, but was told it could take two months to be corrected. We really didn't have that much time, so I just believed God would take care of it. On March 19, two and a half weeks later, it was fixed. All glory to God!

Commit your way to the LORD,
Trust also in Him, and He will do it. (Psalm 37:5 NASB)

At that time, I had been teaching math in a high school in Ohio. In the beginning of March, I realized I would need to transfer my teaching license to Illinois. On March 7, I sent the necessary paperwork for this transfer. Nine days later I received my new certificate and sent my first job application to Chicago. On March 29, we drove six hours to Chicago for my first job interview and six hours back home on the same day. I had a phone interview on April 7, drove to Chicago for another interview on the 9th, and had another phone interview on the 12th.

While all this was going on, friends of ours told another couple that we were moving. We had never met this other couple, but they were believers who had been looking for a house for three years. The husband was a pilot and they were hoping to be strategically placed between two airports. On April 18, we got a call from the wife telling us they would like to come see our house. They came the next day to see it and made us an offer three days later. On April 25, we drew up a contract with a lawyer and closed the sale on June 15. We never even put the house up for sale! God is amazing!

I continued the job search/interview process and God opened the door for the job He had planned for me at a private international French school. I had signed a contract by the end of May and we began to look for houses. We knew nothing about Chicago, so we were relying on the internet to collect information. Mitchell set up a meeting with a realtor and selected a dozen houses for us to visit.

We made a trip to Chicago and stayed with a friend from high school God had reconnected me with the previous summer. As we toured the houses, we felt no peace about them. We prayed and asked God for direction. He led us to increase the radius of our search and raise our price range by faith. As we followed His lead, he led us to the house He had planned for us (Prov 3:5-6).

God guides and He provides. God faithfully opened many doors for us and made everything fall into place according to His good plan for us (Jeremiah 29:11). We had to keep taking the steps of faith, but He led us and made the way where there seemed to be no way.

> *Behold, I will do a new thing,*
> *Now it shall spring forth;*
> *Shall you not know it?*
> *I will even make a road in the wilderness*
> *And rivers in the desert. (Isaiah 43:16)*

Our house was located on the West side of Chicago in a neighborhood full of gangs and drug dealers. We were a minority there and had great peace about where God had placed us. We moved there in the beginning of August as the Lord had said. I began my job as a math teacher later that month. We began to get acclimated to city life and how things worked in our new community. We started getting to know our new neighbors, helped start a block club, and just worked to develop relationships in our community.

God quickly connected us with a church where we were involved in a church plant from the ground up. We served in every area of ministry you can think of. We participated in prayer walks through the city and numerous prayer and planning meetings. We served on the set-up and tear down crew when the church first started and was mobile. Mitchell even made rolling storage cases for all the church equipment. We purchased a box trailer and used our truck to haul all the equipment back and forth every Sunday. We served as deacons and sometimes ran the sound, audio and video. I was the Children's Church Director for a few years and later started a nursey. Basically, whatever the need, we were willing to fill it.

We did many radical outreaches in the community with our church to share the love of Christ. We made care packages for homeless people and spent time visiting them and ministering to them. We organized street cleaning days where we visited various neighborhoods picking up garbage and sharing the gospel. We set up a picnic in our front yard and offered free hotdogs to anyone who walked by. We even baptized a young man in our front yard in a portable tub!

On Wednesday evenings in the summers we would gather with various other churches and spread ourselves around the city streets holding signs which read, "Honk if you love Jesus!" or "Jesus loves you!" Once, we carried a huge cross through the streets and sang worship songs to the Lord. In the winter we went Christmas caroling in neighborhoods where most people didn't even want to drive through. One winter my friend and I gave out free cups of hot chocolate at a train station every Friday morning. Mitchell and I served once a week at a soup kitchen for about a year. We had such a strong desire to show people how much God loves them that we were willing to do anything for Him!

God opened many doors for us to continue on His path for us. We had to continue to take the steps of faith to follow Him. He led, we followed.

Do you believe God will direct your steps? Do you believe He will open doors for you? I believe He will! I encourage you to ask Him to lead, believe that He is and follow Him by taking steps of faith.

Chapter Four: Embracing the Supernatural

Jesus said to him,

"If you can believe,

all things are possible

to him who believes."

(Mark 9:23)

Angel Encounter

Angels are seen all throughout the Bible from Genesis to Revelation. Hebrews 1 tells us that they were created by God as ministering spirits sent forth to minister for those who will inherit salvation. This means that their purpose is to minister to believers.

For He shall give His angels charge over you,
To keep you in all your ways. (Psalm 91:11)

In the New Testament, the Lord sent an angel to Zacharias to inform him that his wife Elizabeth would give birth to John the Baptist (Luke 1:11-20). The Lord sent an angel to Mary to tell her she would miraculously conceive and give birth to the Messiah (Mark 1:26-38). An angel was sent to Joseph to tell him that Mary was carrying the Holy Spirit's

57

child and to go ahead and marry her (Matthew 1:20-21). An angel appeared again to Joseph to warn him to take Mary and Jesus to Egypt to flee from the king Herod (Matthew 2:13). An angel announced the birth of Jesus to the shepherds in Luke 2. Angels came to minister to Jesus after His 40 days of temptation (Matthew 4:11).

In Acts 12 we find the account of Peter's rescue by an angel. He did not really know what was going on at first.

Peter was therefore kept in prison, but constant prayer was offered to God for him by the church. And when Herod was about to bring him out, that night Peter was sleeping, bound with two chains between two soldiers; and the guards before the door were keeping the prison. Now behold, an angel of the Lord stood by him, and a light shone in the prison; and he struck Peter on the side and raised him up, saying, "Arise quickly!" And his chains fell off his hands. Then the angel said to him, "Gird yourself and tie on your sandals"; and so he did. And he said to him, "Put on your garment and follow me." So he went out and followed him, and did not know that what was done by the angel was real, but thought he was seeing a vision. When they were past the first and the second guard posts, they came to the iron gate that leads to the city, which opened to them of its own accord; and they went out and went down one street, and immediately the angel departed from him.

And when Peter had come to himself, he said, "Now I know for certain that the Lord has sent His angel, and has delivered me from the hand of Herod and from all the expectation of the Jewish people." (Acts 12:5-11)

When I got born-again, I began to journal. I am thankful that I did because I had an experience that, like Peter, I didn't quite understand until after it was over. This next account is part of my journal entry for 12-6-2015. This all happened in Oak Park, Illinois.

On 12-5-15, I left the chiropractor's office and was heading to my car. I was walking east on Lake Street to the Pay-to-Park lot by Old Navy. As I was just about to turn to cross the street to get to the parking lot, I noticed an older woman walking east also. She was hunched over and kind of shuffling as she walked. She had on a long winter coat and a scarf. She carried a bad in each hand – a yellow grocery bag in the left and a see-through plastic purse-type bag in the right. I couldn't see her face because of her hunch back and her scarf.

As she passed me, I felt the Spirit say, "Bring her something." I asked in my head, "Is she homeless?" I took a few steps in her direction, then reasoned, "No, I want to get home. I have a lot to do." I turned and headed across the street. As I got to the opposite side the Spirit said, "What will you do if you disobey the Holy Spirit?" My heart sank.in light of my sin and I quickly turned around and crossed back over the street. I said to the Spirit, "What shall I say?! What should I offer to buy her?! This is weird... But I will do it!"

I caught up to her quickly because she didn't walk fast – she shuffled, head down. As I got close to her, I looked in the see-through bag. It had a small stack of paper cups and stuff that looked like garbage or crumpled up paper wrappers. I came up next to her and said, "Hello! How are you today?" I had to keep walking and kind of peer down around to see her

59

face because she never stopped walking and never looked up. She was an African-American woman. She looked older than me but not elderly.

She said, "Oh hello. I am fine, thank you." and kept walking and never looked up. I felt like she didn't really want to be bothered, but I knew I was sent to her so I said, "Well, I just really feel like God told me to come and talk to you. Is there anything you need?" A beautiful smile came across her face though she never looked up and she never stopped walking. "O thank you," she said, "but I am fine." I was persistent, desperate to obey and find out why God sent me to her. "Can I buy you a cup of coffee or something to eat?" "O no thank you," she said, "I am fine."

As we kept walking, I looked down and noticed her feet. Her shoes were not hardly shoes at all. They had soles and a top, but were held together on the sides by threads. I could see her bare feet pushing out the sides with every step. I said, "Well it looks like you could use some new shoes. Can I buy you some shoes?" She said, "O no thank you. I have another pair in my bag. I only have four blocks to go. My feet get sore and I put these on to walk. They are comfortable.

At this point, she and I were crossing Marion St. The red "No cross" hand was up, but she never looked up, so she didn't see it – she just kept shuffle-walking right into the street. I quickly looked around and saw a truck turning toward us. I held up my hand asking him to stop. As we got to the curb I said, "Ok, well can you tell me your name so I can pray for you?" "Irene" she said, "My name is Irene. She never looked up, never stopped walking. I said, "Ok, Irene. Have a blessed day."

As I turned back around to head west to my car I said out loud, "Father God, I pray for Irene. I pray that you would bless her..." For no apparent reason, I turned back around to look at her. She was gone! I mean gone! Impossible!?! I walked back toward where she should be. I had only turned around for four seconds! She was gone! I walked down four storefronts searching for her! In went back up to the first one, the bank. I went inside. She was not there. The second was locked and had a key card access. I pulled on it to make sure it was locked. She would not have had time to put down her bags and dig out a key card!

The next store was a restaurant. I went in. It was empty! By this time, I knew... She was gone! I knew in my heart, but my head was in a spin! "What just happened?!! What just happened?!!" "You saw an angel," said the Holy Spirit. I knew it. I knew it was true, but you don't just walk away from something like that saying, "Cool. I just saw an angel." No! I had a ton of questions! Was it REALLY an angel?! What does "Irene" mean? Why did this happen?! What did it mean?!

As I walked back to the car, I pondered these things as my heart raced! I just said, "Thank You, Lord! Thank You, Lord! Thank You, Lord!" and I thought, "What does Irene mean?"

When I arrived back at our home, I looked up the meaning of her name. I discovered that Irene means peace. God had sent me an angel of peace. It amazes me that I thought she needed something, but God knew exactly what I needed. He sent me an angel of peace in the form a homeless woman.

Angels are real. The Bible even tells us we may encounter them.

> *Let brotherly love continue. Do not forget to entertain strangers, for by so doing some have unwittingly entertained angels. (Hebrews 13: 1-2)*

Do you believe in angels? Do you believe God would use them in your life to minister to you? He did it for me and He will do it for you. I encourage you to believe in angels and live like you believe.

Prayer

Prayer is a supernatural activity. Prayer is simply communicating with God. It involves speaking to Him and listening to His response. It also involves faith since you are talking to someone you cannot see and listening for a voice that is usually not audible to your physical ears.

My prayer life has changed dramatically over the past 20 years. In the beginning, I didn't really know what to say to God because I didn't know Him well. I loved Him with my whole heart from the moment He saved me, but I didn't know His true character and nature.

Consider a baby's ability to communicate. It grows as the child grows in knowledge and understanding. Parents are not angry at the child's lack of communication skills. They just continue to teach and train the child through example and relationship with the child.

Communicating with God is similar. When you first become a Christian, you know God as your Savior. This is how you get born again, you believe in your heart that Jesus died for your sins and that God raised Him from the dead (Rom 10:9). This belief indicates that you acknowledge your need for a Savior. This is the beginning of your relationship with Him. From that moment on, you are invited into communion, fellowship, and relationship with Him. He wants you to know how much He loves you, all that He has done for you, and all that you have access to as His child.

My prayer started as mostly thanking Him for saving me. I still felt a lot of guilt and shame for all I had done in the past. I asked Him over and over to forgive me for all I had done. I have now come to understand that this type of prayer kept me stuck in a false mindset. God had already forgiven me of every sin I had committed and would commit my whole life. He washed all my sins away on the cross with His blood. My part was to receive that forgiveness by believing that it was already done.

then He said, "Behold, I have come to do Your will, O God." He takes away the first that He may establish the second. By that will we have been sanctified through the offering of the body of Jesus Christ once for all. And every priest stands ministering daily and offering repeatedly the same sacrifices, which can never take away sins. But this Man, after He had offered one sacrifice for sins forever, sat down at the right hand of God, from that time waiting till His enemies are made His footstool. For by one offering He has perfected forever those who are being sanctified. But the Holy Spirit also witnesses to us; for after He had said before, "This is the covenant that I will make with them after those days, says the LORD: I will put My laws into their hearts, and in their minds I will write them," then He adds, "Their sins and their lawless deeds I will remember no more." (Hebrews 10:9-17)

In this passage, Jesus clearly reveals God's will and the reason He has come. He came to do God's will which was to take away the first Covenant (Law) and establish the second Covenant (Grace). By that will of God, we who believe in the finished work of the cross *have been* sanctified by the offering of His body *once for all*. He goes on to explain that the priests according to the Old Covenant had to offer repeated sacrifices which could never completely take away sin. Jesus, however, offered one sacrifice for all sins forever. The fact that God raised Him from the dead is evidence that God accepted that payment for all sins. Now Jesus is seated at right hand of the Father because He has no more work to do.

On the cross Jesus declared "It is finished." He was talking about the work God sent Him to do. Jesus came to destroy the works of the devil (1 John 3:8). He accomplished what He was sent here to do (John17:1-4). As the Lord declares in Hebrew 10:17, He remembers our sins and lawless deeds no more. In fact, He declares us righteous. He made us righteous the moment we believed. (Romans 5)

When I received this revelation, I stopped groveling on the floor in prayer declaring how sinful and unworthy I was. I began to humble myself by believing what God said instead of how I felt. I had received the gift of salvation by grace through faith. But, I had not yet received the gift of righteousness in order to reign in life over my feelings and the lies of the enemy.

For if by the one man's offense death reigned through the one, much more those who receive abundance of grace and of the gift of righteousness will reign in life through the One, Jesus Christ. (Romans 5:17)

As I came to the knowledge and better understanding of righteousness, I began to pray differently. We have to put on righteousness by allowing the Word of God to change the way we think and see ourselves.

This I say, therefore, and testify in the Lord, that you should no longer walk as the rest of the Gentiles walk, in the futility of their mind, having their understanding darkened, being alienated from the life of God, because of the ignorance that is in them, because of the blindness of their heart; who, being past feeling, have given themselves over to lewdness, to work all uncleanness with greediness. But you have not so learned Christ, if indeed you have heard Him and have been taught by Him, as the truth is in Jesus: that you put off, concerning your former conduct, the old man which grows corrupt according to the deceitful lusts, and be renewed in the spirit of your mind, and that you put on the new man which was created according to God, in true righteousness and holiness. (Ephesians 4:17-24)

When I began to see myself as righteous, I began to approach God differently. I began to believe that He really had washed my sins away and remembered them no more. This belief changed the way I prayed. I began to approach the throne of grace with boldness and ask the Lord what His plans were (Hebrew 4:16). I began to understand that New Testament prayer is praying WITH God not TO God.

He lives inside of us and loves to commune with us (2 Cor 13:14) and lead us into all truth (John 16:13). He led me into the truth about praying in the Spirit, that is praying in tongues. This changed my life yet again!

Do you believe you can speak to the Creator of the Universe? Do you believe He is listening to you? Do you believe He is talking to you? I encourage you to live like you believe this. Talk to Him, listen for Him and hear what He is saying.

Baptism in the Holy Spirit

I had heard of the Baptism of the Holy Spirit on our trip to Haiti and in various conferences, but it was not taught in the churches we had attended. I was very intrigued by the topic and knew that it was a controversial issue with Christians. I decided to ask Holy Spirit to lead me into truth as He promises to do (John 16:13). If this was a gift that Jesus paid for, I wanted to receive it. He paid way too high a price for me to leave any gift unopened.

At first, I thought that baptism of the Holy Spirit was just praying in tongues. However, the Lord showed me that it is much more than that. John the Baptist declared that Jesus will baptize us with the Holy Spirit and fire.

I indeed baptize you with water unto repentance, but He who is coming after me is mightier than I, whose sandals I am not worthy to carry. He will baptize you with the Holy Spirit and fire. (Matthew 3:11)

66

There are actually three baptisms. Baptize means to place something into something else. In all three cases, there are two people involved, the one doing the baptizing and the one being baptized. The first baptism occurs when you are born-again. At this moment, the Holy Spirit baptizes you into the Body of Christ.

For by one Spirit we were all baptized into one body—whether Jews or Greeks, whether slaves or free— and have all been made to drink into one Spirit. (1 Corinthians 12:13)

We see Jesus speaking to the woman at the well about this "drink" we are offered. Jesus asks the woman to give Him a drink. She replies, "How is it that You, being a Jew, ask a drink from me, a Samaritan woman?" (John 4:9). He tells her in the next verse, "If you knew the gift of God, and who it is who says to you, 'Give Me a drink,' you would have asked Him, and He would have given you living water." The water that He is referring to is the Holy Spirit who comes to live inside of you the moment you are born-again. This gift is for your personal relationship with Him. It is a fountain springing up from inside you for eternal life, which is knowing God (John 17:3).

Jesus answered and said to her, "Whoever drinks of this water will thirst again, but whoever drinks of the water that I shall give him will never thirst. But the water that I shall give him will become in him a fountain of water springing up into everlasting life." (John 4: 13-14)

The second baptism is water baptism. One person submerges another person into water. It is the burial service for the old man and has great spiritual significance. Though your old sinful man died the day you got saved, (2 Cor 5:17) we need to take a step of faith to show the world in the physical realm what took place in the spiritual realm. John the Baptist was baptizing with water and Jesus commanded the disciples to do the same.

Go therefore and make disciples of all the nations, baptizing them in the name of the Father and of the Son and of the Holy Spirit, (Matthew 28:19)

The third baptism is baptism in the Holy Spirit. It may occur before, during or after water baptism. Jesus is the baptizer and a believer is the one getting baptized. Baptism in the Holy Spirit is a gift and a promise from God. Like the other gifts, they must be received through faith. God, who is love, does not demand His own way (1 Cor 13:5). He will never force anyone to be baptized in the Holy Spirit and He will never force anyone to speak in tongues. He offers the gift and gives the gift immediately when a believer asks.

"So I say to you, ask, and it will be given to you; seek, and you will find; knock, and it will be opened to you. For everyone who asks receives, and he who seeks finds, and to him who knocks it will be opened. If a son asks for bread from any father among you, will he give him a stone? Or if he asks for a fish, will he give him a serpent instead of a fish? Or if he asks for an egg, will he offer him a scorpion? If you then, being evil, know how to give good gifts to your children, how much more will your heavenly Father give the Holy Spirit to those who ask Him!" (Luke 11:9-13)

Here Jesus is explaining that the gift of the Holy Spirit is a GOOD gift. Every good and perfect comes from the Lord (James 1:17) and He is no respecter of persons (Rom 2:11). He will give it to you if you ask. I had asked, but I did not understand all that I have explained here. So, I did not know how to receive the gift. God's people are destroyed for lack of knowledge (Hosea 4:6). We access the promises and power of God through the knowledge of Him (2 Peter 1:2-4). So, as I gained more knowledge, I realized that God had given me the gift of baptism in the Holy Spirit the first time I asked. It was then that I believed and received the gift of tongues, my personal prayer language.

While Peter was still speaking these words, the Holy Spirit fell upon all those who heard the word. And those of the circumcision who believed were astonished, as many as came with Peter, because the gift of the Holy Spirit had been poured out on the Gentiles also. For they heard them speak with tongues and magnify God. (Acts 10:44-46)

Some believers today have not heard of the baptism in the Holy Spirit. That was the case for me when I first got saved. It was also the case for some believers in Ephesus.

And it happened, while Apollos was at Corinth, that Paul, having passed through the upper regions, came to Ephesus. And finding some disciples he said to them, "Did you receive the Holy Spirit when you believed?" So they said to him, "We have not so much as heard whether there is a Holy Spirit." And he said to them, "Into what then were you baptized?" So they said, "Into John's baptism." Then Paul said, "John indeed baptized with a baptism of repentance, saying to the people that they should believe on Him who

*would come after him, that is, on Christ Jesus." When they
heard this, they were baptized in the name of the Lord
Jesus. And when Paul had laid hands on them, the Holy
Spirit came upon them, and they spoke with tongues and
prophesied. Now the men were about twelve in all. And he
went into the synagogue and spoke boldly for three months,
reasoning and persuading concerning the things of the
kingdom of God. (Acts 19:1-8)*

Many believers are afraid of praying in tongues or
claim that it is of the devil. That is interesting to me because
when I was still a sinner (not yet saved), I never spoke in
tongues. In fact, I have never met an unsaved person who
claims to speak in tongues. Also, Paul, who wrote more of the
New Testament than any other writer, professed to speak in
tongues more than anyone else. He also encouraged us to not
be ignorant of the gifts (1 Cor 12:1).

*I thank my God I speak with tongues more than you
all; yet in the church I would rather speak five words with
my understanding, that I may teach others also, than ten
thousand words in a tongue. (1Cor 14:18-19)*

Paul makes it very clear in this verse that in a corporate
setting, he would rather speak in a language that others could
understand for the purpose of teaching them. In private,
however, praying in tongues has many personal benefits. It
facilitates your intimacy with God (1 Cor 14:2 and 1 Cor
14:14). Praying in tongues edifies us (1 Cor 14:4) and draws
wisdom from your spirit to your mind (1 Cor 14:2). It builds
up our faith and keeps us in the love of God (Jude 20-21).
Praying in tongues will bring us into rest (Isaiah 28:11-12).

70

This type of prayer helps us to draw on the Spirit and pray the perfect will of God.

> *Likewise the Spirit also helps in our weaknesses.*
> *For we do not know what we should pray for as we ought,*
> *but the Spirit Himself makes intercession for us with*
> *groanings which cannot be uttered. Now He who searches*
> *the hearts knows what the mind of the Spirit is, because He*
> *makes intercession for the saints according to the will*
> *of God. (Romans 8:26-27)*

It was the beginning of 2016 when Mitchell and I really embraced these truths and began praying in tongues. That's when things really took off!

Do you believe God has more gifts for you than you have already opened? Are you willing to consider that some of your beliefs are not true? If so, get ready to be set free! I encourage you to believe that the baptism in the Holy Spirit is for you today! Simply believe that it is, ask for it, and receive it by faith!

Healing from Disease

After about three and a half years in Chicago, the Lord led us to a different church. Though we had enjoyed all the fellowship and outreach at the first church, the Lord had other things He wanted to teach us. At the new church Mitchell got involved with a ministry that went out on the streets on Friday nights to minister to pimps and prostitutes. I got involved in some women's Bible studies. We made some very close friendships at this church. We also learned so much more about the gifts of the Spirit and healing.

When I was a little girl, I had headaches and stomach aches all the time. As I got older, the headaches turned into migraines and the stomach aches turned into constant "going to the bathroom". I would get brain fog and woke up most mornings feeling like I got hit by a truck. By the time I was in my 20s, I had learned to live with this as my normal. I had constant soreness in my lower abdomen and it was very painful to the touch.

Over the years I had gone to doctors for various other symptoms like constant abdominal pains, cramping, extreme fatigue. I was put on kidney medication, has exploratory surgery on my female parts and was put on various medicines. In my 30's, I was hospitalized a few times and even had my gall bladder removed even though they could not find any cause for my symptoms and pain.

In February of 2012 I was hospitalized for 9 days. My body had shut down as if I had had a stroke. None of the tests or scans that were run revealed the source of the problem. During the last two days of my stay there, a weekend doctor encouraged me to take my health into my own hands and do some research online. She said that just because they couldn't figure out what was wrong, didn't mean there was nothing wrong. She said there was so much more in the medical realm that was unknown than known.

Looking back, I see that God had sent this woman to minister to me. My health issues had been a source of shame and guilt for decades. I was told I was seeking attention and not really sick. People didn't know how bad it was because I learned to deal with it silently. So, when this doctor said these words to me, it empowered me to believe that there truly was something wrong and something I could do about.

The day I was released from the hospital, the Lord led me to the answer within three clicks on the internet. It was called Celiac disease which is severe gluten intolerance. As I read the account of people with the disease, I literally read my life history. The interesting thing about Celiac is that it is incurable, but controllable with diet. I did all the research to find out what I could not eat and cut all of those foods out of my diet. I also had to eliminate nuts, dairy, beef, pork and soy for two years because my intestines were so damaged.

My health started to get better and I was able to slowly add the foods back into my diet that did not contain gluten. I still had to be extremely cautious of eating at restaurants or friends' houses. All seemed to be going well until the summer of 2016. Food that did not even contain gluten started making me feel sick again. The symptoms all started coming back and got worse and worse. Finally, one Friday in August, I was so sick that I went to bed at noon and said, "Lord, I will not eat again until you tell me what to do."

When the Lord moved us to our 2nd church in Chicago, we began to learn about healing. We had seen some miraculous healing on our trip to Haiti in 2012 and we believed God could heal if He wanted to. What we did not know at the time is that God not only CAN heal, but He desires for you to be healed EVERY time. One of the names of God is Jehovah-Rapha, the God Who heals.

To understand God's will in healing, and every other issue, we must look at Jesus. Jesus was the full revelation of God the Father.

> *He is the image of the invisible God, the firstborn*
> *over all creation. (Colossians 1:15)*

In Hebrews 1:3, it says Jesus is "the brightness of *His* glory and the *express* image of His person". He Himself says He only did what He saw the Father do. He demonstrated the Father's will for us.

> *Then Jesus answered and said to them, "Most*
> *assuredly, I say to you, the Son can do nothing of Himself,*
> *but what He sees the Father do; for whatever He does, the*
> *Son also does in like manner. (John 5:19)*

Jesus never made any person sick. He only healed. Consider these verses.

> *He sent His word and healed them,*
> *And delivered them from their destructions. (Psalm 107:20)*

> *Bless the LORD, O my soul, And forget not all His*
> *benefits: Who forgives all your iniquities,*
> *Who heals **all** your diseases, (Psalm 103:2-3)*

> *how God anointed Jesus of Nazareth with the Holy*
> *Spirit and with power, who went about doing good and*
> *healing **all** who were oppressed by the devil, for God was*
> *with Him. (Acts 10:38)*

> *And Jesus went about all Galilee, teaching in their*
> *synagogues, preaching the gospel of the kingdom, and*
> *healing **all** kinds of sickness and **all** kinds of disease among*

*the people. Then His fame went throughout all Syria; and they brought to Him **all** sick people who were afflicted with various diseases and torments, and those who were demon-possessed, epileptics, and paralytics; and He healed them. (Matthew 4:23-24)*

*But when Jesus knew it, He withdrew from there. And great multitudes followed Him, and He healed them **all**. (Matthew 12:15)*

*When the sun was setting, **all** those who had any that were sick with various diseases brought them to Him; and He laid His hands on **every one** of them and healed them. (Luke 4:40)*

In Genesis 1 and 2, we see all that God created. After everything He created, He declared it "good". After He created man, He declares it "very good". Sickness is not listed as something God created and deemed "good". John 10:10 tells us very clearly that God is not the author of sickness. The devil is.

The thief does not come except to steal, and to kill, and to destroy. I have come that they may have life, and that they may have it more abundantly. (John10:10)

The purpose of sickness is to kill your physical body. Even a common cold can kill you. Sickness does not fit into the category of "abundant life" that Jesus came to give you. It is not a "good and perfect gift" which is the kind of gifts God gives (James 1:17). Jesus came to destroy the works of the devil (1 John 3:8) and He accomplished what He came here to do (John 17:4).

75

God created your body with the ability to heal itself. You are born with an immune system that attacks and fights off sickness and disease the moment it tries to enter your body. Your body also has the ability to produce antibodies when new viruses try to come in. Your blood clots to heal a wound when you get cut. God created healthy food and medicinal plants to support His plan for us to be physically and mentally healthy.

I did not know these truths when I was a child nor when I was first born-again. When I got saved, I was taught that God *could* heal if He wanted to. However, as I continued in the Word and in relationship with God, I began to see His perfect will for my life is to be healthy, healed and whole all the time. God brought other believers into my life who believed in the healing power of God and His will for healing. Like many people, I believed I had to wait for God to heal me. The problem in believing that was that He ALREADY healed me 2000 years ago on the cross.

who Himself bore our sins in His own body on the tree, that we, having died to sins, might live for righteousness—by whose stripes you were healed. (1 Peter 2:24)

On August 27, 2016 I woke up feeling like I had been hit by a truck. The day before was the day I had declared I would not eat again until God showed me what to eat. It was Saturday and women's Bible study was that morning. I determined I would go regardless of how I felt. I can't remember what the pastor was teaching, but I know it was not healing. A woman in the back of the room asked her a question about pain in her feet. Her answer was about to change my life forever.

Here is what she said: "It's not God's will for you to be sick."

That simple, profound statement of truth exploded in the core of my being! In that very moment, I believed with my whole heart that this sickness that had tormented me from childhood was NOT of God. I BELIEVED that it was not His will. At that very moment I RECEIVED complete healing!

It was like the day I got saved and the day I decided God is good and the day I touched Mitchell's knee for the first time. I knew that I knew that I knew I was healed. Holy Spirit bore witness in my spirit. I was overwhelmed with God's love for me. I had connected in my heart to a truth that set me free! (John 8:31-32)

> *And whatever things you ask in prayer, believing, you will receive." (Matthew 21:22)*

The key is in what you believe. I had asked many times before that day in prayer to be healed, but what I was believing was not truth. That day, I believed the truth and it set me free from a lifetime of sickness! God had already healed me 2000 years ago on the cross and I just believed and received His gift! All glory to God!

Do you believe that God can heal you? Do you believe He wants you healed, healthy and whole? Do you believe He already healed you 2000 years ago? I invite you to believe it and receive healing in your body right now.

PART III: WONDERS

God also bearing witness

both with signs and wonders,

with various miracles,

and gifts of the Holy Spirit,

according to His own will.

(Hebrews 2:4)

The Greek word for "wonders" is *teras*. It means a miraculous wonder done to elicit a reaction from onlookers; an extraordinary event with its supernatural effect left on all witnessing it. Wonders are for others to see.

Christians are not called to live secret lives. As members of the Body of Christ, we are called to unity and to be seen by the world around us. We are called to live in such a way that others see us for the purpose of bringing God glory.

Let your light so shine before men, that they may see your good works and glorify your Father in heaven.
(Matthew 5:16)

God wants all people to be saved and come to know Him (1 Tim 2:3-4). His plan for this to happen includes us believers. He sent Jesus to make Himself known and to give

79

us an example of how to live a Spirit-empowered life on this earth. Jesus declared before He went to the cross that He finished His work on the earth (John 17:4). Then, He sent us (believers) into the world as the Father sent Him (John 17:18). This commission was not just for the disciples of that day, but for all who would believe in Him even to this day (John 17:20).

What an honor and privilege to be a co-laborer with Christ (1 Cor 3:9)! He is the same yesterday, today, and forever (Heb 13:8), and is therefore, still bearing witness with signs, wonders and miracles today. We are His Body on the earth; His hands, feet, eyes, ears and mouths. He will continue His work as He has promised. He worked with the apostles and wants to work with you.

And through the hands of the apostles many signs and wonders were done among the people. And they were all with one accord in Solomon's Porch. (Acts 5:12)

Do you believe this? I do! I invite you to believe it too!

Chapter Five: Abundant Life

The thief does not come except

to steal, and to kill, and to destroy.

I have come that they may have life,

and that they may have it more abundantly.

(John 10:10)

Fasting

At our first church in Chicago, we learned about fasting. Each January, we would begin the year with a 21-day fast. Fasting is a spiritual discipline seen in the Old and New Testaments. Fasting must be accompanied with prayer because the purpose of fasting is to position your heart to receive what the Lord is desiring to give you. When you fast, you are denying your flesh in a declaration that God's will is more important to you than your body's desire for food. You are seeking to hear His voice.

Moses fasted on the mountain when he went to receive the Ten Commandments (Ex 34:28). Elijah fasted 40 days and 40 nights (1 Kings 19:7-8). The Jews fasted in the book of Esther when they faced destruction (Esther 4:16). Daniel, Ezra and his people, the Ninevites, and others in the Old

Testament fasted in various circumstance with the purpose of seeking the Lord. Jesus Himself fasted in the wilderness before He faced the three temptations of the devil (Matt 4:2).

All that Jesus did was for an example for us. He not only demonstrated fasting but also instructed us on how to fast. We are instructed not to fast to be seen by man. Fasting is a heart issue. Like all other things we do, God cares more about the "why" behind the "what". The reason you are fasting matters to God. We are called to do all things for His glory (Col 3:23).

"Moreover, when you fast, do not be like the hypocrites, with a sad countenance. For they disfigure their faces that they may appear to men to be fasting. Assuredly, I say to you, they have their reward. But you, when you fast, anoint your head and wash your face, so that you do not appear to men to be fasting, but to your Father who is in the secret place; and your Father who sees in secret will reward you openly. (Matthew 6:16-18)

In the book of Acts, we see the apostles and disciples fasting and praying as they sought guidance from Holy Spirit. As they were fasting they heard Holy Spirit's direction. After hearing, they obeyed.

As they ministered to the Lord and fasted, the Holy Spirit said, "Now separate to Me Barnabas and Saul for the work to which I have called them." Then, having fasted and prayed, and laid hands on them, they sent them away. (Acts 13:2:2-3)

After four years of doing the 21-day fasts, Mitchell and I adopted a lifestyle of fasting. We decided to fast one day a week every week. Some weeks the Lord would lead us to continue our fast even into two or three days. It was during one of these fasts in 2016 that Mitchell was given more clarity on the land vision. He knew the Lord was calling us to the south-west part of Michigan. The more we fasted and prayed in the Spirit, the more clarity we received.

One day in June as we were fasting, Mitchell was at work and heard a voice say, "Fish Farm." He looked around to see who it was, but no one was there. He continued on with his business and heard it again, "Fish Farm." He looked around and again saw no one. He then realized it was Holy Spirit speaking to him. So, he asked Him what He meant.

Over the next few days and weeks, the Lord revealed many more details about the ministry He was calling us into. He told Mitchell it would be in Michigan and even highlighted the area for him. Mitchell began to look for property in that area. The Lord revealed to me that the name of the ministry came from Matthew chapter 4.

Then He said to them, "Follow Me, and I will make you fishers of men." They immediately left their nets and followed Him. (Matthew 4:19-20)

Have you ever considered Biblical fasting? Do you believe that it is still purposeful today? I encourage you to ask Holy Spirit to reveal truth to you about fasting. I invite you to believe in the purpose and power of fasting and take a step of faith in that area!

Desires of Your Heart

In October of 2016, I had another life-changing encounter with God. I was still teaching math at the French school in Chicago and still pursuing deeper relationship with God every day. I loved Him with my whole heart and had a strong desire to know Him more. Every morning I rose early to have hours alone with Him, His Word and Holy Spirit.

Delight yourself also in the LORD,
And He shall give you the desires of your heart. (Psalm
37:4)

As I spent time with Him over the years, I discovered the desires of my heart changing. When I began my career teaching math at 23 years old, I had determined that I would never retire. I believed that I was going to teach math until the day I died. I loved teaching, I loved teenagers, and I loved math. It all made sense to me according to my beliefs at that time. However, after I believed in God and began spending time with Him, my mind began to change. I began to think differently and the desires of my heart started to change.

And do not be conformed to this world, but be transformed
by the renewing of your mind, that you may prove
what is that good and acceptable and perfect will of God.
(Romans 12:2)

When you get born-again, you become a new creation in your spirit man (2 Cor 5:17). Your soul, which includes you mind, must be trained how to think as this new creation. The Word of God will do the training if you allow Him.

For the word of God is living and powerful, and sharper than any two-edged sword, piercing even to the division of soul and spirit, and of joints and marrow, and is a discerner of the thoughts and intents of the heart. (Hebrews 4:12)

Romans 12:2 tells us that we must not remain conformed to the world's way of thinking, feeling and behaving. Hebrews 4:12 explains that the soul and spirit are divided by the Word of God. When we think like Him, we will act like Him. We find further instructions for the mind in Ephesians 4.

that you put off, concerning your former conduct, the old man which grows corrupt according to the deceitful lusts, and be renewed in the spirit of your mind, and that you put on the new man which was created according to God, in true righteousness and holiness. (Eph 4:22-24)

Notice in this passage that your new man was created righteous and holy. This was according to God. You already ARE righteous and holy. It is your mind that needs to "put on" the new man by believing this new reality. You will live out whatever you believe, whether lies or truth. God has given us His Word and His Spirit so that we may know Him and show Him to the world around us. However, only those who chose to enter into the relationship with Him are the ones who will show Him correctly.

The Bible is not a Christian obligation. If you believe this lie, you will never experience the fullness of life that Jesus paid for you to experience (John10:10). The Word of God is an invitation to intimacy with a good and loving Father who so desires the best for you. His Word is profitable for you in four specific ways.

All Scripture is given by inspiration of God, and is profitable for doctrine, for reproof, for correction, for instruction in righteousness, that the man of God may be complete, thoroughly equipped for every good work. (2 Tim 3:16-17)

The Word of God will teach you, show you what you are believing wrong, correct your thinking, and train you IN righteousness. Recall from Ephesians 4 that you were created righteous and holy by God. Now according to 2 Timothy 3, you need to be trained in your new self, your new identity, so that you will be fully equipped for every good work.

Notice the benefit found at the end of Romans 12:2 of allowing the Word of God to transform your mind. You will be able to discern His good, acceptable and perfect will for you. This is what Paul is talking about in Philippians 2 when he instructs believers to work out their own salvation with reverence to the Lord.

Therefore, my beloved, as you have always obeyed, not as in my presence only, but now much more in my absence, work out your own salvation with fear and trembling; for it is God who works in you both to will and to do for His good pleasure. (Phil 2:12-13)

Paul is talking about soul salvation which is mind-renewal. The blood of Jesus saved you from your sins and gave you the power to be born again. After you are saved, Holy Spirit IN you works with you to renew your mind through the Word in order to do His good pleasure. His good pleasure will become your good pleasure as you delight yourself in Him (Psalm 37:4).

This is exactly what happened to me. In October of 2016, I came home from work and flopped myself into a chair. I was dissatisfied with my life even though we were serving the Lord like crazy. Serving God and knowing Him are two very different things. I had such a strong desire to KNOW him, that I cried out to Him that day with arms crossed and pouty face. I said, "GOD! Something has to give! I want to KNOW you more! Show me what to do!" I felt like a pop can that was all shook up, full of pressure, and about to explode.

After my little tantrum, I fell asleep in the chair. I woke up a little while later and heard in my spirit, "Go to Bible college." WHOA!!! It was like the pop top had been flipped open! Joy was exploding from my heart! I said, "YES!! That's an awesome idea!! Where should I go??" He said, "Ask Pastor Lynn where she went." Pastor Lynn was my dear friend who led the women's Bible study I attended at our church.

I often laugh at myself when I tell God how good His ideas are. I mean think about it, who could come up with a better idea than the Creator of the universe who formed and shaped you in your mother's womb (Psalm 139) and knows the plans He has for you (Jer 29:11)?? So, I called Pastor Lynn and asked her where she went to college.

She informed me she had gone to Charis Bible College and was telling me all about the teachers, the various locations and the different options for attending. Before we hung up the phone, I was enrolled in my first class. I decided to take online classes for the first year since it was already the end of October and I was still working full time.

I was so excited that I texted my dad to tell him I had just started Bible college. He texted back, "What do you get?" I responded, "What do you mean?" After a few more texts, I realized what he was asking. He was asking what type of degree or certification I would receive. I hadn't even thought to ask! I just wanted to KNOW God more and this was His answer for that desire.

I discovered that the college offered a two-year program to become a licensed minister. With the on-line option, I could pace myself. I decided to complete one lesson a day, which would allow me to finish the first year by the end of August 2017. That would enable me to start the 2nd year at the Chicago extension school in September. I was going to finish this school year teaching math at the French school, quit my job, and attend Bible college full time in the fall. That was my plan.

It is good idea to plan in pencil and keep the eraser available for God.

A man's heart plans his way,
But the LORD directs his steps. (Prov 16:9)

When I cried out for "help", God gave me a husband. When I cried out to know Him more, He sent me to Bible College. Both of these gifts were, and continue to be, exceedingly more than I could have ever imagined!

Now to Him who is able to do exceedingly
abundantly above all that we ask or think, according to the

power that works in us, to Him be glory in the church by Christ Jesus to all generations, forever and ever. Amen. (Eph 3:20-21)

Do you believe He will give you the desires of your heart? Are you willing to allow His Word to change your mind and lead you on the path of His perfect plan for you? I invite you to believe it!

Steps of Faith

One month after I started at Charis, Mitchell believed he had found the property God wanted for us. He had been perusing land for sale for years knowing that one day we would be living in the vision God had given him. He came across a property in Michigan that looked perfect in his eyes. It had a house, over 80 acres, and multiple outbuildings that looked perfect for so many of the things God had shown him. We decided to visit the property and pray over it. This was a step of faith.

We drove out to Michigan and walked the property. As we went through each building, we envisioned what we would be able to do in each one according to God's plan. We were so excited about the idea of our vision coming to life!

It looked perfect, except for one little thing - I had this "check" in my spirit. It just didn't feel quite right. I was tempted to ignore it, but it was still there. I didn't want fear to stop God's plan, so I didn't say anything about it. A few of our family members met us at the property to see it with us. Before we left, we all held hands in a circle and prayed to the

Lord. We surrendered ourselves to His will and His perfect plan for us and asked Him to reveal it in Jesus' name.

Now this is the confidence that we have in Him, that if we ask anything according to His will, He hears us. And if we know that He hears us, whatever we ask, we know that we have the petitions that we have asked of Him.
(1 John 5:14-15)

The house was up for sale by online auction. The day of the auction, Mitchell and stayed home from work to fast and pray. We had prayed beforehand and believed the Lord had given us a dollar amount to not go beyond. It was all we thought we could afford. As the auction began and continued, our hearts were pounding with excitement.

We were eager to see what would happen. We believed that if this was our property, we were about to win it in the auction. We watched as the bidding went up and up. We continued to pray and thank God for His perfect plan. Finally, the bidding reached the maximum amount we had committed to offer. We looked at each other as if to say, "What now?"

It was one of those cross-roads moments where you have to make a split decision. If we went higher, we could put ourselves in a financial bind. If we didn't go higher, we would lose the property and possibly abort God's plan for us. At least that's what we believed at the time.

I went into another room to pray in tongues. When I came back in I told Mitchell I felt peace to raise our offer $10,000 but no more. He said he also felt peace with that. So, we increased our bid and waited prayerfully.

90

And let the peace of God rule in your hearts, to which also you were called in one body; and be thankful. (Colossians 3:15)

Peace is one of the greatest gifts Jesus has given us (John 14:27). Jesus Himself is our peace (Eph 2:14), so peace lives inside of us believers. We are told to go forth in joy and be led by peace (Is 55:12). As Christians, peace is our GPS. We need to follow peace. So, in the moment of decision, Mitchell and I called out to God and He answered from inside our hearts with His peace.

Very quickly after we placed our last offer, the bidding shot up and we "lost" the property. For a moment, we just sat still. There were many thoughts to entertain if we so chose. Mitchell felt disappointment and was experiencing sadness. He had believed with his whole heart that this was the property.

These are moments of reality in life. You have a dream, a plan, a vision. You take a step of faith that you truly believe God led you to take, and then you seem to hit a brick wall. In that moment, you have a crisis of faith. Questions rise up like: "What do I believe now?", "Did I miss God?", "Did God not come through?", "Did I just kill the vision?", "What just happened?"

I began to recall the visit to the property and remembered the "check" in my spirit. Holy Spirit was bringing to remembrance things He had taught me (John 14:26). He reminded me that He had a good plan for us to prosper us and not to harm us (Jer 29:11). He reminded me that His plans never fail (Is 14:24). He works all things together for good (Rom 8:28). He reminded me that we had prayed and agreed on the property for His will to be done.

Joy rose up in my heart and I said, "Mitchell, if we thought this was the perfect property, God has one EVEN BETTER than this!!" He is able to do exceeding abundantly beyond what we can ask or think (Eph 3:20). He doesn't think like us. His ways are higher than ours.

"For My thoughts are not your thoughts,
Nor are your ways My ways," says the LORD.
"For as the heavens are higher than the earth,
So are My ways higher than your ways,
And My thoughts than your thoughts. (Isaiah 55: 8-9)

Faith rose up in both of us and we praised the Lord for His perfect plan. We thanked Him for protecting us from getting the wrong property. We walked out of that day in hope, trusting the Lord for something more.

Not even a week later, God led Mitchell to the place He had truly planned for us. Mitchell had seen this certain property about six months before. He had felt drawn to it, but seeing the asking price, he deleted it from the emails thinking we could never afford it. The owner had been trying to sell the land for some years, but it had not sold. Because of this, he had sectioned the 130+ acres into three parcels. We calculated that in our financial situation, we could afford two of the three parcels. We scheduled an appointment with the realtor to see the property in January, 2017. This was another step of faith.

We had not yet gone to see the property in person and had decided not to make any decision or offer until after our

21-day fast. The property fit perfectly into the vision God had given Mitchell. I was pondering on how to make it work with only two parcels of land. The third parcel was about 50 wooded acres of rolling hills. It was part of the vision, but we couldn't afford it all. I just kept pondering and trying to figure out how to make it work.

One morning during my time with the Lord, He spoke these words in my heart, "Believe for all of it." Oh, how my heart leapt with joy! I texted Mitchell at work, "God said we need to believe for all the land!" He said "Amen!"

Faith goes beyond what you can see. Faith believes beyond what you can do on your own. We did not need faith to acquire two parcels. We had the down payment, the credit score and the finances for two parcels. We could not, however, qualify for or afford all three. God invites us to walk by faith (2 Cor 5:7). Faith is the currency we use to purchase what we cannot afford in the natural realm.

Now faith is the substance of things hoped for, the evidence of things not seen. (Hebrews 11:1)

Faith rises up when you hear the voice of God (Rom 10:17). We had been praying and fasting and were expecting an answer. I had heard Him and believed. You can pray and fast and still miss it if you do not BELIEVE that He is answering.

But without faith it is impossible to please Him, for he who comes to God must believe that He is, and that He is a rewarder of those who diligently seek Him. (Hebrews 11:6)

Once you pray, fast, listen and hear Him, you then need to obey. We had been given a directive from the Lord to believe for all of the land. We decided to obey Him and believe for all of it in spite of our lack in the physical realm. We took steps in the physical realm according to that belief.

If you are willing and obedient,
You shall eat the good of the land; (Isaih 1:19)

We continued to fast, pray, listen and obey over the next six months. Many obstacles came to make it look like things were not going to work out. One example was the day before we were supposed to close the deal, the insurance company I had been working with for weeks informed me they could not insure the house. It would be impossible to acquire another company in one day and we could not close the deal without homeowner's insurance.

The Lord had led me to meditate Matthew 17:20 for weeks before this happened. He is always giving us what we need before we need it. He is in the business of equipping His saints (Eph 4:12).

So Jesus said to them, "Because of your unbelief; for
assuredly, I say to you, if you have faith as a mustard seed,
you will say to this mountain, 'Move from here to there,' and
it will move; and nothing will be impossible for
you. (Matthew 17:20)

When the email came from the insurance company stating that they could not insure us, I literally spoke out loud by faith, "Mountain, be thou removed in Jesus' name!" I had no doubt in my heart that this was just a ploy from the enemy to stop God's plan. I also believed that this was not impossible

94

for God! I had already seen mountains moved when He moved us from Ohio to Chicago in five and a half months. I had NO doubt. One hour later, I had insurance for the house from another company. All glory to God! He keeps His Word!

We closed on the property in June, and moved into the house a month later. Obstacles in the physical realm are no problem for God. As believers we have the God-given authority in Christ to command them out of our way. God will lead you to take steps of faith in His plan for you. We are not to be intimidated by anything that appears to be in the way. We walk by faith, not by sight (2 Cor 5:7).

But we are not of those who shrink back and are destroyed, but of those who have faith and preserve their souls. (Hebrews 10:39 ESV)

Are you believing for something beyond your ability? Is God moving in your heart to step out in faith for something that is impossible? I invite you to fast, pray, listen and obey. Believe that He is and that He is a rewarder of those who diligently seek Him (Heb11:6).

Direction

When we had started the process of acquiring the land, I was excited, but also had questions for God. I knew He had directed me to go Bible college and I had planned to quit my job at the end of the school year and attend full time at the Chicago extension. Now, we were moving to Michigan. I asked God, "How is this going to work?" I also couldn't understand how we could get the biggest mortgage we had ever had and both quit our jobs.

Holy Spirit led me to look up Charis locations in Michigan. At that time, there was only one which had the 2nd year program available and it was only one and a half hours from our property. I called the school and found out that they were starting a new hybrid program the very next school year. In this program, students could complete most of their classes online and attend in person only two Saturdays per month. It was perfect for me. I now believe that God had planned this all along.

> *A man's heart plans his way, But the LORD directs his steps. (Prov 16:9)*

As Christians, we often hesitate to devise a plan for fear of "missing God". Fear is not from God (2 Tim1:7), and it paralyzes us. Proverbs 16:9 says man plans, but God directs his steps. This means that it is perfectly fine to create a plan and trust God to direct the steps. If we delight ourselves in the Lord, He will place His desires in our heart (Psa 37:4). If the desires of your heart fit under the umbrella of God's will, you can believe and trust that it is Him directing your path. God's will for all mankind is that they would be saved and come to know Him.

> *For this is good and acceptable in the sight of God our Savior, who desires all men to be saved and to come to the knowledge of the truth. (1 Timothy 2:3-4)*

As you devise a plan, check with Holy Spirit to see if it fits into His desire for all men to be saved and come to come to know Him. My plan was to quit my job and go to Bible college in Chicago. This would help me know Him more and be able to teach others about Him. That lined up with His will.

After I made the plan, I had to take steps of faith in that plan. God promises to direct our steps. Faith without corresponding action is dead faith. This is what James is talking about in chapter 2.

What does it profit, my brethren, if someone says he has faith but does not have works? Can faith save him? If a brother or sister is naked and destitute of daily food, and one of you says to them, "Depart in peace, be warmed and filled," but you do not give them the things which are needed for the body, what does it profit? Thus also faith by itself, if it does not have works, is dead. But someone will say, "You have faith, and I have works." Show me your faith without your works, and I will show you my faith by my works. You believe that there is one God. You do well. Even the demons believe—and tremble! But do you want to know, O foolish man, that faith without works is [h]dead? Was not Abraham our father justified by works when he offered Isaac his son on the altar? Do you see that faith was working together with his works, and by works faith was made perfect? And the Scripture was fulfilled which says, "Abraham believed God, and it was accounted to him for righteousness." And he was called the friend of God. You see then that a man is justified by works, and not by faith only. Likewise, was not Rahab the harlot also justified by works when she received the messengers and sent them out another way? For as the body without the spirit is dead, so faith without works is dead also. (James 2:14-26)

Steps of faith are a result of believing God. As I took the steps, I had to trust Him to direct them. As I took steps in MY plan, God directed those steps into HIS plan. As His plan was unfolding before my eyes, I then had to choose to follow His plan and let go of mine.

There are many plans in a man's heart, Nevertheless the LORD's counsel—that will stand. (Proverbs 19:21)

I started at Charis Ann Arbor in September, 2017. I also took a fulltime position teaching math at a local high school. The Lord had told Mitchell to quit working and dedicate his time to building up the property the way the Lord had shown him. This was a huge transition for Mitchell since he had been an electrician in Ohio for twenty-five years and in Chicago for five. He truly loves the Lord and believed in the vision the Lord had given him. Because of this love and belief, he chose to dedicate his time to fulfill God's plan.

If you love Me, keep My commandments. (John 14:15)

During my second year in Bible college, the Lord showed me He also wanted me to quit my job and "work" full time for Him. I still could not understand how we could both quit our jobs and continue to pay our mortgage and bills. But God had built me up to believe He would provide (Phil 4:19). He had led me to trust that He had the best plan (Jer 29:11) and was leading us in that plan. He had worked in me to believe that I did not need to understand, but just needed to acknowledge Him in all my ways (Prov 3:5-6).

The desires in my heart had completely changed over the 16 years since I had gotten saved. I no longer had any desire to teach math. I just wanted to teach the Word. I graduated from Bible college in May of 2018 and received my ministry license. It was quite a celebration for me, but not nearly as exciting as the freedom I was experiencing in knowing God like I had never known Him before.

And this is eternal life, that they may know You, the only true God, and Jesus Christ whom You have sent. (John 17:3)

What is God directing you to do? Have you devised a plan? I encourage you to a create a plan then take a step trusting and believing God to direct your steps.

Chapter Six: Living in the Call

I, therefore, the prisoner

of the Lord, beseech you

to walk worthy of the calling

with which you were called,

(Ephesians 4:1)

Career to Calling

The Lord continued to reveal more and more about His plan for us and the ministry. I quit my job by faith and ended a career that had lasted twenty-four years. I had spent four years in college earning a Bachelor's degree and two more years earning a Master's degree. I had invested time and money to take over thirty hours beyond my Master's to reach the highest level on the pay scale. I had spent time and money to complete courses to transfer my teaching license from Ohio to Illinois and again from Illinois to Michigan. In the eyes of the world, I had invested a huge portion of my life and finances into this career of being a math teacher. But God.

But what things were gain to me, these I have counted loss for Christ. Yet indeed I also count all things

101

loss for the excellence of the knowledge of Christ Jesus my Lord, for whom I have suffered the loss of all things, and count them as rubbish, that I may gain Christ (Philippians 3:7-8)

The Word of God had begun a good work in me (Phil 1:6) and had continued to work in me (Phil 2:13) to bring about His perfect plan for me. My part was to keep seeking and abiding and believing Him. I had to live like I believed what He was saying. I had to live like I believed He loves me and has a perfect plan for my life in Him.

I worked the entire summer putting together and submitting everything that was needed to apply for a 501c3 non-profit organization. Thankfully, friends of ours had connected us with an organization to help me with this. God always supplies what we need (Phil 4:19). On my 47th birthday, August 27, 2018 Fish Farm Ministries, Inc. was born. I had also worked all summer with my sister and my nephew to get a website up and running. It was launched in the beginning of October that same year. All glory to God!

When I had started Bible college two years before, my heart was just to know Him more. I had never imagined that I would be the head pastor of a ministry. God knew the plan He had for me. He had definitely done immeasurably more than I had asked or imagined (Eph 3:20). And He was not done!

Mitchell and I truly didn't know how to start or run a ministry. Our hearts' desire was to know God. When we first moved to Chicago, we knew God as our Savior. We knew we were going to live in eternity with Him because He had saved us. We knew Him as Lord and desired to serve Him. However, God is more than just a Savior and a Lord. He is a Father, a Friend, a Deliverer, a Healer, the Lover of your Soul. He is a Husband, a Redeemer, a Restorer, a Rewarder, and so much more! He desires for us to know Him intimately. He desires for that intimacy to continue and deepen every day of our lives. His call to us as believers is to KNOW Him and the power of His resurrection (Phil 3:10).

As He led my husband and me out of our careers, He led us into our calling. Our calling is to know Him and be one with Him as Jesus was one with Him.

"I pray for them. I do not pray for the world but for those whom You have given Me, for they are Yours. And all Mine are Yours, and Yours are Mine, and I am glorified in them. Now I am no longer in the world, but these are in the world, and I come to You. Holy Father, keep through Your name those whom You have given Me, that they may be one as We are. (John 17:9-11)

As we came to know Him, we discovered the plan He had for us specifically to live in communion with Him every moment of every day. The ministry He led us into was not our primary calling. It was part of our opportunity to know Him as Provider, Restorer, Healer, Redeemer, Rewarder, etc. and to lead others into knowing Him more.

God led me to enroll in an optional 3rd year program at Charis Bible college called Leadership. This track was a combination of the Business and Ministry tracks offered at the main campus in Colorado. It was exactly what I needed to

103

know Him more and to continue taking steps in our ministry. God does not call the equipped. He equips the called.

> *And we have such trust through Christ toward God. Not that we are sufficient of ourselves to think of anything as being from ourselves, but our sufficiency is from God, who also made us sufficient as ministers of the new covenant, not of the letter but of the Spirit; for the letter kills, but the Spirit gives life. (2 Corinthians 3:4-6)*

In September of 2018, I started leading Bible studies in our home and at our church. The groups grew in number of attendees throughout the year. I was also doing one-on-one discipleships in my home, on the phone and over Skype. In August of 2019, I accepted a position as a Chaplain at a local Christian school where I was also able to teach 10th grade Bible classes for two years. God was opening doors for me to share the revelations and teachings the Lord had given me through Bible college and in our time alone.

> *You therefore, my son, be strong in the grace that is in Christ Jesus. And the things that you have heard from me among many witnesses, commit these to faithful men who will be able to teach others also. (2 Timothy 2:1-2)*

I had stepped out of my career, being a math teacher, and into my calling, knowing Him and teaching others about Him.

> *The LORD will fulfill his purpose for me; your steadfast love, O LORD, endures forever. Do not forsake the work of your hands. (Psalm 138:8 ESV)*

Do you believe God has a calling and specific purpose for your life? Are you living in your career or your calling? I encourage you to ask the Lord to show you a step of faith you can take to begin walking in your calling.

The Two Shall become One

Marriage is an amazing gift from God. Many people do not understand the covenant relationship they enter into when they say "I do." Marriage was God's plan from the beginning. When God created everything in Genesis 1, He declared everything "good". When He created man, He declared him "very good". The first thing we see in the Word that God that He declares "not good" was that man was alone. He, of course, had the perfect solution for this.

And the LORD God said, "It is not good that man should be alone; I will make him a helper comparable to him." (Genesis 2:18)

God's plan from the beginning was for one man to be married to one woman and that they would live together in unity. He decrees that the man shall leave his father and mother and be joined to his wife, and they shall become one flesh (Genesis 2:24). God desires that all believers walk together in unity of belief (1 Pet 3:8). This is especially important in marriage.

Can two walk together, unless they are agreed? (Amos 3:3)

Mitchell and I both loved the Lord with our whole hearts and sought His will in all things. However, during my years in Bible college, God revealed some truths to me that Mitchell had not yet been exposed to. I wanted to teach him, but I was not called to be his teacher. This caused a slight undercurrent of tension, which is not God's desire in marriage. I prayed and asked the Lord to reveal these truths to Mitchell as He had done for me. I was confident that God desired us to walk in unity and would fulfill His plan for our marriage.

Now this is the confidence that we have in Him,
that if we ask anything according to His will, He hears us.
And if we know that He hears us, whatever we ask, we know
that we have the petitions that we have asked of Him. (1 John
5: 14-15)

I graduated from the 3rd year of Bible college in May 2019. One morning, about a month later, the Holy Spirit woke Mitchell up and said, "Mark 4:14". Mitchell woke me up and told me what had happened. He then went to get his Bible and turned the pages to the verse.

The sower sows the word. (Mark 4:14)

As he pondered with the Lord about what He meant, he realized God was calling him to Bible college. This was not only an answer to my prayer for unity in our marriage, but also an answer to Mitchell's prayer to know God more. By this time, there was another Charis location only one hour from our home. We decided to go to Charis Interest Day in Grand Rapids, Michigan.

As we were sitting at the college that day listening to the founder, Andrew Wommack, speaking on a live-stream, he said, "and in Mark 4:14 it says the sower sows the Word." Mitchell elbowed me, we looked at each other and just smiled. He enrolled in the hybrid program that day and started classes in September of 2019. I volunteer as a facilitator and got to go with him to school the two Saturdays each month that he went.

Through this experience, God solidified His truth in both of our hearts and brought us into unity in our beliefs. It was not that we disagreed before, it was that there were truths we had not experienced together yet. In marriage, both spouses will not necessarily come to know the same truths at the same time. God desires an intimate individual relationship with each spouse. He knows what every person needs and is leading each one into the truth he/she needs in each moment as that person is willing to be led (John 16:13). At the same time, God desires unity in marriage.

But from the beginning of the creation, God 'made them male and female.' 'For this reason a man shall leave his father and mother and be joined to his wife, and the two shall become one flesh'; so then they are no longer two, but one flesh. Therefore what God has joined together, let not man separate." (Mark 10:6-9)

Because of the desires of our hearts to know Him more, God led us each individually to Bible college. God used Bible college to strengthen our individual relationships with Him, which in turn strengthened our relationship with each other. We are now able to sharpen each other in a godly way.

As iron sharpens iron, So a man sharpens the countenance of his friend. (Proverbs 27:17)

We do not always agree on everything, but we trust the Holy Spirit to teach us (John 14:26). We also know that it is not our job to convince the other of truth. That is the job of the Holy Spirit (John 16:13). When you truly believe this, and stop trying to change your spouse, you will experience a supernatural flow of love and grace in your marriage like never before. Whenever we believe and submit to the way God designed for us to live, peace and joy prevail.

I press toward the goal for the prize of the upward call of God in Christ Jesus. Therefore let us, as many as are mature, have this mind; and if in anything you think otherwise, God will reveal even this to you. Nevertheless, to the degree that we have already attained, let us walk by the same rule, let us be of the same mind. (Phil 3:14-16)

Wives are not called to correct and teach our husbands. We are called to submit as unto the Lord. Husbands are called to love your wife as Christ loved the church and gave Himself up for us.

Wives, submit to your own husbands, as to the Lord. For the husband is head of the wife, as also Christ is head of the church; and He is the Savior of the body. Therefore, just as the church is subject to Christ, so let the wives be to their own husbands in everything. Husbands, love your wives, just as Christ also loved the church and gave Himself for her, that He might sanctify and cleanse her with the washing of water by the word, that He might present her to Himself a glorious church, not having spot or wrinkle or any such thing, but that she should be holy and without blemish. So husbands ought to love their own wives as their own bodies;

*he who loves his wife loves himself. For no one ever hated
his own flesh, but nourishes and cherishes it, just as the
Lord does the church. For we are members of His body, of
His flesh and of His bones. "For this reason a man shall
leave his father and mother and be joined to his wife, and
the two shall become one flesh." This is a great mystery, but
I speak concerning Christ and the church. Nevertheless let
each one of you in particular so love his own wife as himself,
and let the wife see that she respects her husband.
(Ephesians 5: 22-33)*

God's desire for you is that you would be one with
Him. His desire in your marriage is that you and your spouse
become one. When this happens, you, your spouse, and Jesus
become a three-strand cord which is nearly impossible to
break.

*Two are better than one, Because they have a good
reward for their labor.
For if they fall, one will lift up his companion. But woe to
him who is alone when he falls,
For he has no one to help him up. Again, if two lie down
together, they will keep warm;
But how can one be warm alone? Though one may be
overpowered by another, two can withstand him. And a
threefold cord is not quickly broken. (Ecclesiastes 4:9-12)*

Do you believe God has a perfect plan for marriage?
Do you believe He will lead you in His plan for you? I
encourage you to live like you believe it!

The Abundant Life

God had brought Mitchell and I together in 2008 and led us to the mission field in 2010. He had given Mitchell the vision of land in 2012, and then called us to Chicago. There He grew us and brought more clarity to the vision. God led us to Michigan in 2017. Fish Farm Ministries was birthed in August, 2018. In November of 2019, we hired Amish builders to put up the first ministry building. They built the outside of the structure in 9 days!

It was amazing to watch the vision the Lord had placed in Mitchell's heart start to manifest in the physical realm. He had led us and directed our steps, and there in front of our eyes, we saw the wonder of the confirmation of what God had said (Heb 2:4). Over time, we learned that we were experiencing the law of sowing and reaping.

Let him who is taught the word share in all good things with him who teaches. Do not be deceived, God is not mocked; for whatever a man sows, that he will also reap. For he who sows to his flesh will of the flesh reap corruption, but he who sows to the Spirit will of the Spirit reap everlasting life. And let us not grow weary while doing good, for in due season we shall reap if we do not lose heart. Therefore, as we have opportunity, let us do good to all, especially to those who are of the household of faith. (Galatians 6:7-10)

The spiritual realm is governed by spiritual laws, just as the physical realm is governed by physical laws of nature. A person does not have to believe in God or even know these laws for them to govern his/her life. God has put them all into place for the welfare of mankind.

Gravity is a good example of a physical law. A baby does not know the law of gravity, but she will fall to the floor if she rolls off a changing table. A person can say, "I don't believe in the law of gravity." but he will fall to the ground if he jumps out of a window. Without the law of gravity, we would fly off the earth into outer space and die.

Physical and spiritual laws exist because God created them for us to be able to enjoy abundant life with Him. The law of sowing and reaping (Gal 6:8) mandates that you will reap (gather the produce) from what you have sown (planted). If you plant watermelon seeds, you will grow watermelons. If you plant grass seed, you will grow grass. There are other variables that come into play such as good soil (Mark 4), sunlight and water.

The law of sowing and reaping also applies in your body. If you sow healthy food and healthy habits into your body, you will reap health. If you sow junk food and bad habits, you will reap health problems. There are other components involved including time. Just like seeds planted in the physical realm take time to grow, so the law of sowing and reaping happens over time.

Mitchell and I experienced the law of sowing and reaping in our finances. We were always generous givers and believed that we could not out-give God. We believed that God had given us all that we had (Jas 1:17), so we gave generously with cheerful hearts. We expected God to do abundant miracles with the financial seed we sowed even if we never knew of them. As we gave, we continued to receive an abundance back to us (Luke 6:38). We always had enough for ourselves and extra to give away. This caused us to be

111

even more thankful to God and even more generous in our
giving for His glory.

> *But this I say: He who sows sparingly will also reap
> sparingly, and he who sows bountifully will also reap
> bountifully. So let each one give as he purposes in his
> heart, not grudgingly or of necessity; for God loves a
> cheerful giver. And God is able to make all grace abound
> toward you, that you, always having all sufficiency in
> all things, may have an abundance for every good work. As it
> is written: "He has dispersed abroad, He has given to the
> poor; His righteousness endures forever. "Now may He
> who supplies seed to the sower, and bread for food, supply
> and multiply the seed you have sown and increase the fruits
> of your righteousness, while you are enriched in everything
> for all liberality, which causes thanksgiving through us to
> God. (2 Corinthians 9:6-11)*

The law of sowing and reaping also applies in
relationships (Gal 6:9). If you are kind to others, you will reap
kindness. If you are rude to others, you will reap rudeness. If
you meditate on sad things, you will reap depression. If you
meditate on things above (Phil 4:8), you will reap joy and
peace. If you sow abundantly into your relationship with God,
you will reap an abundance of peace and joy. You will reap a
prosperous soul (1 John 1:2) overflowing with love and all
fruit of the Spirit (Gal 5:22-23). Peace will become the ruler
of your heart and thankfulness will abound. You will be living
like you believe that all the promises of God are for you (2
Cor 1:20).

> *And let the peace of God rule in your hearts, to which also
> you were called in one body; and be thankful. Let the word*

of Christ dwell in you richly in all wisdom, teaching and admonishing one another in psalms and hymns and spiritual songs, singing with grace in your hearts to the Lord. And whatever you do in word or deed, do all in the name of the Lord Jesus, giving thanks to God the Father through Him. (Colossians 1:15-17)

Mitchell and I learned of these spiritual laws as we continued in the Word (John 8:31-32) and allowed Holy Spirit to teach us (John14:26). As we believed in these laws, we chose to obey them. In doing so, we experienced more and more of the abundant life Jesus died for us to have (John 10:10).

God had led us to educations and jobs throughout our entire lives. He had led us to Bible college and instructed us to quit our jobs. He led us to create a ministry and showed us the specific place to start it. He had given us promises to stand on each and every step of the way. Our abundant life did not begin the day we acquired the ministry property. It did not begin the day the first ministry building went up. It had begun the day each of us gave our heart to the Lord and believed in Jesus. And this abundant life has continued and increased as we have sown into our relationship with God.

This is the abundant life that Jesus died for you to experience here on this earth. Jesus came to destroy the works of the devil (1 John 3:8). He accomplished what He came here to do (John 17:4). The abundant life is knowing him and the power of His resurrection (Phil 3:10). When you desire to know God and live a supernatural abundant life, you must sow into your relationship with God.

113

Do you believe this abundant life is available for you? I encourage you to believe, and live like you believe. Sow your time into your relationship with God and you be amazed at what you reap!

On the Horizon

When the pandemic hit in 2020, our ministry began to explode. What the devil meant for evil, God surely used for good (Gen 50:20). We began to focus on building the outside structures and planted our garden. We took our Bible studies virtual and began making more Bible study videos for our website. We continued hosting intimate discipleships in our home and also on-line. We partnered with our church and hosted a four-day youth camp for teens that summer. We offered teen Bible studies on Wednesday nights in July and August. We also hosted a men's discipleship weekend in October.

At the time Mitchell graduated Bible college in May 2021, God had brought others into the ministry with us. We had six online Bible studies with participants reaching from the east to the west coasts of the United States and down to Texas and Georgia. We continued working on the ministry building and the garden and started the woodshop as the Lord guided and provided. Mitchell and I continued to agree with all the Lord had shown us and told us (John 16:13).

"Again I say to you that if two of you agree on earth concerning anything that they ask, it will be done for them by My Father in heaven. (Matthew 18:19)

114

On February 28, 2017 I had written in my journal, "I know this farm will bless and minster to thousands upon thousands of people! Lord, have your way! Direct our every step! All for your glory!" I still believe that to this day. We have already been able to bless hundreds of people and more keep coming!

On the horizon we see more lives touched. We see more people saved, set free, and coming to know God. We see more youth camps, discipleship weekends, and Bible studies. We see more buildings, greenhouses, a wedding venue, and a woodshop. We see missionary housing and mission trips. Most importantly, we see ourselves immersed in the love of God, growing deeper in intimacy with Him each and every day. He will continue what He started.

being confident of this very thing, that He who has begun a good work in you will complete it until the day of Jesus Christ; (Philippians 1:6)

We see Him leading our steps and others with us on the path of life (Psa 16:11). We see us all enjoying Him and His creation. We see triumphant lives lived with gratitude for the One who created us, lives in us and loves us dearly. We see others being drawn to the fragrance of Him through us.

Now thanks be to God who always leads us in triumph in Christ, and through us diffuses the fragrance of His knowledge in every place. For we are to God the fragrance of Christ among those who are being saved and among those who are perishing. To the one we are the aroma of death leading to death, and to the other the aroma of life leading to life. And who is sufficient for these

115

things? For we are not, as so many, peddling the word of God; but as of sincerity, but as from God, we speak in the sight of God in Christ. (2 Corinthians 2:14-17)

God is able to do exceedingly abundantly above all that we ask or think according to His power which is at work in you (Eph 3:20). You have to envision what only God can do. You must imagine with God what is impossible for man.

But Jesus looked at them and said to them, "With men this is impossible, but with God all things are possible." (Matthew 19:26)

Never settle for less than what God can do. God will use your life as an opportunity to show His glory. He will strengthen you, help you, and uphold you through it all (Is 41:10). God is for you, He will provide (Rom 8:31-32). When it is God's plan, it cannot be overthrown (Acts 5:38-39).

What is on the horizon for you? I invite you to ask God for a God-sized vision. Do you believe that He will show you things to come and lead you on His path? I invite you to live like you believe!

Epilogue/Conclusion

God wants you to know Him (John 17:3). He is an intimate God who loves you so deeply and wants you to receive His love and all He paid for through Christ's death on the cross. God wants to reveal Himself to you. This is my prayer for you:

Therefore I also, after I heard of your faith in the Lord Jesus and your love for all the saints, do not cease to give thanks for you, making mention of you in my prayers: that the God of our Lord Jesus Christ, the Father of glory, may give to you the spirit of wisdom and revelation in the knowledge of Him, the eyes of your understanding being enlightened; that you may know what is the hope of His calling, what are the riches of the glory of His inheritance in the saints, what is the exceeding greatness of His power toward us who believe, according to the working of His mighty power which He worked in Christ when He raised Him from the dead and seated Him at His right hand in the heavenly places, far above all principality and power and might and dominion, and every name that is named, not only in this age but also in that which is to come. (Ephesians 1:15-21)

What do you truly believe about God? What do you really believe about Jesus? I encourage you to explore the answers to these questions. You will live out whatever you truly believe in you heart (Prov 23:7).

117

I pray you will ask Holy Spirit to teach you all things (John 14:26) and lead you into all truth (John16:13). He loves to do this! He is ready, willing and able. I pray you will be able to answer Jesus like Simon Peter in Matthew 16.

He said to them, "But who do you say that I am?" Simon Peter answered and said, "You are the Christ, the Son of the living God." Jesus answered and said to him, "Blessed are you, Simon Bar-Jonah, for flesh and blood has not revealed this to you, but My Father who is in heaven. (Matthew 16:15-17)

I pray that you will live like you believe every word written in His Word and spoken in your heart. May you become His disciple indeed (John 8:31-32), experience the abundant life He came to give you (John 10:10), and never stop taking one step of faith after another in Jesus's name. Amen.

But be doers of the word, and not hearers only, deceiving yourselves. For if anyone is a hearer of the word and not a doer, he is like a man observing his natural face in a mirror; for he observes himself, goes away, and immediately forgets what kind of man he was. But he who looks into the perfect law of liberty and continues in it, and is not a forgetful hearer but a doer of the work, this one will be blessed in what he does. (James 1:22-25)

Acknowledgments

I want to give thanks and all the glory to Holy Spirit who inspired and wrote this book. I also want to thank my husband, Mitchell for loving God first and me second, and for always believing in Christ in me. Thank you to my family and friends who have supported us throughout the years in so many ways. I also want to thank my closest friends who knew about this book and prayed for me. You are worth more than rubies, diamonds and pearls.

I love you all with all my heart.

About the Author

Erin Gutowski graduated in 1994 from Kent State University in Kent, Ohio with a Bachelor's degree in Math and a minor in education. She earned her Master's Degree in the Art of Education from Marygrove College in Detroit, Michigan in 2001. She received a ministry license from Charis Bible college in 2018 and graduated from their 3rd year Leadership program in 2019.

Erin and her husband Mitchell have been missionaries in various countries including Haiti, Sri Lanka, El Salvador, the United States, Romania, Bulgaria, Nicaragua, and the Dominican Republic. They now co-pastor Fish Farm Ministries, Inc. in Battle Creek, Michigan. Their ministry is currently touching lives across the globe the for the glory of God.

To see more of the vision and mission of Fish Farm Ministries, Inc., visit their website at www.thefishfarm.org.

Made in the USA
Las Vegas, NV
07 April 2022